The Constitution, the Courts, and the Quest for Justice

American Enterprise Institute for Public Policy Research

A DECADE OF STUDY OF THE CONSTITUTION

How Democratic Is the Constitution?

Robert A. Goldwin and William A. Schambra, editors

How Capitalistic Is the Constitution?

Robert A. Goldwin and William A. Schambra, editors

How Does the Constitution Secure Rights?

Robert A. Goldwin and William A. Schambra, editors

Separation of Powers: Does It Still Work?

Robert A. Goldwin and Art Kaufman, editors

How Federal Is the Constitution?

Robert A. Goldwin and William A. Schambra, editors

How Does the Constitution Protect Religious Freedom?

Robert A. Goldwin and Art Kaufman, editors

Slavery and Its Consequences:
The Constitution, Equality, and Race

Robert A. Goldwin and Art Kaufman, editors

The Constitution, the Courts, and the Quest for Justice

Robert A. Goldwin and William A. Schambra, editors

The Constitution, the Courts, and the Quest for Justice

Robert A. Goldwin
and William A. Schambra
editors

American Enterprise Institute for Public Policy Research
Washington, D.C.

Available in the United States from the AEI Press, c/o Publisher Resources Inc., 1224 Heil Quaker Blvd., P.O. Box 7001, La Vergne, TN 37086-7001. Distributed outside the U.S. by arrangement with Eurospan, 3 Henrietta Street, London WC2E 8LU England.

This book is the eighth in a series in AEI's project "A Decade of Study of the Constitution," funded in part by grants from the National Endowment for the Humanities. A full list of the titles appears on the series page.

A somewhat revised version of chapter 2 was published as "How Does the Constitution Establish Justice?" *Harvard Law Review* (March 1988).

Library of Congress Cataloging-in-Publication

The Constitution, the courts, and the quest for justice / Robert A.
    Goldwin and William A. Schambra, editors.
            p.   cm. — (AEI studies ; 491)
        ISBN 0-8447-3691-0 (alk. paper). — ISBN 0-8447-3692-9 (pbk. :
alk. paper)
            1. United States—Constitutional law.   2. Courts—Unites States.
        3. Judicial review—United States.   I. Goldwin, Robert A., 1922–
    . II. Schambra, William A.   III. Series.
        KF4550.A2C655   1989
342.73—dc20
[347.302]   89-17659
                                                                                            CIP

AEI Studies 491

Printed in the United States of America

Contents

The Editors and the Authors

ROBERT A. GOLDWIN is resident scholar and director of constitutional studies at the American Enterprise Institute. He served in the White House as special consultant to the president of the United States and, concurrently, as adviser to the secretary of defense. He has taught at the University of Chicago and Kenyon College and was dean of St. John's College in Annapolis, Maryland. He is the author of *Why Blacks, Women, and Jews Are Not Mentioned in the Constitution, and Other Unorthodox Views* (forthcoming) and the editor or coeditor of more than a score of books, including *How Democratic Is the Constitution?*, *How Capitalistic Is the Constitution?*, *How Does the Constitution Secure Rights?*, and *How Federal Is the Constitution?*

WILLIAM A. SCHAMBRA is communications adviser to the director, Office of Personnel Management. He was a resident fellow at the American Enterprise Institute and codirector of constitutional studies at AEI. He is coeditor, with Robert A. Goldwin, of *How Democratic Is the Constitution?*, *How Capitalistic Is the Constitution?*, and *How Does the Constitution Secure Rights?* and author of "The Roots of the American Public Philosophy" and "Progressive Liberalism and American Community."

WALTER BERNS is the John M. Olin University Professor at Georgetown University and an adjunct scholar at the American Enterprise Institute. A political scientist, he is the author of a number of books and articles dealing primarily with the Constitution of the United States, including *Freedom, Virtue and the First Amendment* (1957) and *Taking the Constitution Seriously* (1987). He was a member of the National Council on the Humanities and has served on the American delegation to the United Nations Commission on Human Rights.

ABRAM CHAYES is the Felix Frankfurter Professor of Law at Harvard Law School. Previously Mr. Chayes served as legal adviser at the U.S. Department of State. Mr. Chayes is the author of numerous articles and books on legal subjects, including *The International Legal Process* (1968) and *The Cuban Missile Crisis, International Crisis and the Role of Law* (2nd ed., 1987).

HARRY M. CLOR is professor of political science and the former director of the Public Affairs Conference Center at Kenyon College. Mr. Clor has written numerous scholarly articles on constitutional themes and is the author of *Obscenity and Public Morality: Censorship in a Liberal Society* (1969).

ROBERT K. FAULKNER is professor of political science and chairman of the department at Boston College. He is the author of *The Jurisprudence of John Marshall* and *Richard Hooker and the Politics of a Christian England* and articles on political philosophy and American legal and political thought.

HENRY G. MANNE is dean of George Mason University School of Law and director of the University's Law and Economics Center. He has written or cowritten a dozen books, including *Insider Trading and the Stock Market*, and more than a hundred articles. He has been a leader in the development of law and economics scholarship.

GARY L. McDOWELL is resident scholar at the Center for Judicial Studies where he also serves as articles editor of the center's publication, *Benchmark*. Mr. McDowell was a fellow at Harvard Law School and at the Woodrow Wilson International Center for Scholars and has held positions in the U.S. Department of Justice and the National Endowment for the Humanities. He is the author of numerous articles on the Constitution and constitutional law and several books, including *Curbing the Courts: The Constitution and the Limits of Judicial Power* (forthcoming) and *The Constitution and Contemporary Constitutional Theory* (1986).

MICHAEL J. PERRY is the Stanford Clinton, Sr., Research Professor at Northwestern University School of Law. He has also taught at Ohio State, Yale, and Tulane. He is the author of many articles on constitutional law and theory and two books: *The Constitution, the Courts, and Human Rights* (1982) and *Morality, Politics, and Law* (1988).

Preface

Among the purposes for which "we the people . . . [did] ordain and establish this Constitution," according to the Preamble, was the intention "to establish Justice." The Constitution does not say just how this is to be done, but from the beginning of the republic, Americans have tended to associate the idea of justice with the rule of law and with a strong, effective, independent system of judges and courts whose purpose is to interpret and enforce the law, including the Constitution itself.

Today, however, the role of the courts in our constitutional system is the source of considerable legal, academic, and political controversy. Much of that controversy turns on the question, How should the courts understand and promote justice?

According to one view, justice is done when the courts observe and enforce the civil and political rights and procedures spelled out in the Constitution—nothing more, and nothing less. As Publius notes in *Federalist* No. 78, the "inflexible and uniform adherence to the rights of the Constitution, and of individuals . . . [is] indispensable to the courts of justice."

In this understanding, the Constitution is the fundamental law of the land, reflecting the "consent of the governed," which alone is the foundation of free and legitimate government. As with any law or regulation, the meaning of the fundamental law is to be sought in the intention of those who framed and ratified it. The establishment of justice thus involves the courts in a search for, a literal interpretation of, and a strict adherence to the original intention of the framers of our constitutional system of rights and procedures.

Another contemporary school of thought suggests that this is a radically insufficient view of the way justice is served in the American political system. According to this second understanding, the intention of the framers is difficult, if not impossible, to discern and so cannot serve as a guide for judicial behavior. At any rate, many of the Constitution's provisions are vague and open-ended, serving as an invitation to the courts to look beyond the four corners of the document for its meaning.

Finally, in this view, justice in the life of the nation cannot be understood as something set forth once and for all by the Constitutional Convention of 1787. Our society has changed dramatically since then, and our understanding of what justice requires has developed and matured. The courts, according to this argument, have been and continue to be instrumental in the evolution of our collective sense of morality and justice. Indeed, the judiciary's chief function is to lead the way toward new, more advanced, and more enlightened understandings of justice by interpreting the Constitution and the laws in light of the best moral and philosophic thought of our time—especially the idea of the "equal dignity" of individuals.

Advocates of the "original intention" approach reject this view because, they maintain, it encourages the substitution of the judge's personal and arbitrary views of justice for those duly ratified by the people in the text of the Constitution itself. The idea of equal dignity, in this view, is particularly pernicious, because in the hands of the courts, it has been used to level distinctions and institutions that a free society requires to survive, especially the family and private property.

Thus is joined the contemporary debate over the constitutional role of the courts and their place in the American understanding of justice. The essays in this volume explore these alternative views, as well as others that seek to incorporate elements of each. One of our authors, for instance, maintains that the courts must indeed occasionally reach beyond the text of the Constitution for justice to be done. The principles they should consult, however, are not to be found in contemporary moral or philosophical theory but rather are embedded in the design and structure of the Constitution itself. That structure points toward a certain conception of a good polity or regime. The courts, in this view, should act with the basic principles of the American political regime in mind.

The essays in this volume (written originally for a conference cosponsored by the American Enterprise Institute and the U.S. Department of Justice by prominent scholars from a variety of disciplines and reflecting a wide range of viewpoints) are designed to give the reader the full flavor of the debate over the judiciary's role in the establishment of justice. As will become apparent, the contemporary controversy in fact has roots deep in the American political tradition, going back to the earliest days of the republic. The controversy also necessarily leads us to reflect on some of our most important and enduring national commitments: to justice, individual rights, popular rule, private property, and the family. What begins as an inquiry into the role of the courts becomes an inquiry into the fundamental principles of the regime. If the reader begins to appreciate the deeper concerns raised by the central question of this volume, then these essays will have served their purpose.

ROBERT A. GOLDWIN
WILLIAM A. SCHAMBRA

1
The Politics of
Original Intention

Gary L. McDowell

*When a strict interpretation of the Constitution, according to the
fixed rules which govern the interpretation of laws, is abandoned,
and the theoretical opinions of individuals are allowed to control its
meaning, we have no longer a Constitution; we are under the
government of individual men, who for the time being have power to
declare what the Constitution is, according to their own views of
what it ought to mean.*

> JUSTICE BENJAMIN R. CURTIS
> *Dred Scott* v. *Sandford*
> (Dissenting Opinion)

The Constitution was born in controversy and thus has it lived. From
the time of the ratification struggle and the debates between the
Federalists and the Anti-Federalists, to disputes between the Jefferso-
nians and the Federalists, to the debate between Chief Justice John
Marshall and President Andrew Jackson, to the crisis of the house
divided and the impassioned rhetoric of Abraham Lincoln and Stephen A. Douglas, throughout our history the question of how to
interpret the Constitution has animated and divided public opinion.
The reason, of course, is that the Constitution is a document explicitly
designed to order our politics. Politically, therefore, a great deal hangs
on the peg of interpretation.

Today we are engaged in a great and robust public debate over
how to interpret the Constitution, a debate that at one level is part of
the great tradition of this country. But at another level the current
debate, the debate over what Attorney General Edwin Meese III has
called a jurisprudence of original intention, is unlike the other great
constitutional debates throughout our history. For in those others the
issue was typically between what used to be called strict constructionists and loose constructionists. The question for them was
how to read the Constitution. Today, the debate is between those

1

dubbed interpretivists and others rather more oddly named noninterpretivists. The question today is not so much how to read the Constitution as *whether* to read the Constitution.

The current controversy over interpreting the Constitution—between those who support a jurisprudence of original intention and the followers of a morally evolutionary approach to interpretation—is no longer a detached academic squabble. It is a political battle of the first order. The battle is nothing less than a fierce fight over what theory of constitutionalism will guide this nation into the twenty-first century.

In a way the current debate, though different in substance from the earlier scuffles, testifies to the continuing relevance, the continuing political importance of the Constitution. This is a very important point, because the reason the Constitution remains relevant to us at this bicentennial juncture is that the framers sought to create a Constitution that (in their words) would be "paramount," "fundamental," and that would "last forever" or, at the very least, "last for ages."[1] This they thought they could do, this they thought they had done, by designing the document not in light of the transitory circumstances peculiar to their time but in light of what they deemed, and what history and political philosophy had shown to be, the permanent attributes of human nature, both its virtues and its vices.

The framers believed, as Alexander Hamilton put it in *Federalist* No. 1, that they could design a government through "reflection and choice" and not leave their political fate to the ravages of "accident and force." They were not utopian; they knew that they were "yet remote from the happy empire of perfect wisdom and perfect virtue." Thus they sought to create a government, as Madison said, "to be administered by men over men"—a sturdy republican government for ordinary people engaged in ordinary pursuits. Their goal was a government that was sufficiently powerful to control the governed yet so designed that it was obliged to control itself. The end they sought was liberty through law.[2]

The key to their design was a written Constitution of clear and common language that would create and limit the institutions of the government. They knew the necessity of providing for a government that would be able to meet the exigencies that time would surely bring but to be able to do so within the context of a limited Constitution of enumerated powers. The point was to create a system of government that would be able to reconcile the inevitability of change in political affairs with principles deemed permanent. The written Constitution, duly ratified by the governed, would be, as Hamilton put it, the "fundamental law."[3]

For that generation, then, the Constitution represented what the

Declaration of Independence had posited as the only legitimate foundation for political power—the consent of the governed. As Hamilton said in *Federalist* No. 78, the Constitution, properly understood, was nothing less than the embodiment of "the intention of the people."[4] Constitutional interpretation therefore carries with it a special obligation to refer to that intention of the people, to the Constitution's original intention.

At the most basic level, a jurisprudence of original intention is a recourse to the basic principles underlying the Constitution. The need is to take seriously the text of the Constitution and the principles that undergird that text, what Hamilton called in *Federalist* No. 9 the new "science of politics." As Hamilton put it:

> The regular distribution of power into distinct departments—the introduction of legislative balances and checks—the institution of courts composed of judges holding their offices during good behavior—the representation of the people in the legislature by deputies of their own election—these are either wholly new discoveries or have made their principal progress towards perfection in modern times. They are means, powerful means, by which the excellencies of republican government may be retained and its imperfections lessened or avoided.[5]

To this catalog the framers added two more: the idea of an extensive commercial republic with a hustling and bustling multiplicity of interests that would undercut the natural propensity of popular governments to tend toward majority faction and tyranny; and the judicious modification of the federal principle, so dividing sovereignty that the Constitution provided "in strictness neither a national nor a federal constitution; but a composition of both" making it "neither wholly federal nor wholly national." By such a division between the nation and the states, they sought to provide "a double security . . . to the rights of the people."[6]

These institutional contrivances, as James Madison described them, were designed to render popular government good government in spite of itself.[7] These are what Paul Bator has called the "postulates of good government."[8] These constituted a system of "successive filtrations" whereby all the opinions and passions and interests of the people could be "refined and enlarged"; this system was designed to transform ordinary quantitative majority rule into a qualitative majority rule.[9] It was in this substantive design of "a government with powers to act and a structure to make it act wisely and responsibly . . . that the security of American civil and political liberty" was thought by the founders to lie.[10]

Today the critics of a jurisprudence of original intention seek to

3

perpetuate several basic myths that serve their political purposes. First, they argue that a jurisprudence of original intention is tied to the particular circumstances of the late eighteenth century, that it is "static."[11] This is manifestly untrue. The founders thought, as I have just suggested, that they were designing a document for the future as much as, indeed more than, for their present. They were young men of a continental vision.[12] Their obligation, as they said in the Preamble, was to their posterity as well as to themselves. Thus the Constitution that generation drafted and ratified was a forward-looking document not meant to shackle America to that time but to release it to become all that it could—indeed has—become. They built not on particular circumstances but on general principles; it is to those principles and not to those circumstances that a jurisprudence of original intention urges us to recur.

Second, it is argued that a jurisprudence of original intention is nothing more than an appeal to personal, subjective notions of particular founders, the argument being that the founders, not unlike statistics, can be manipulated to prove nearly anything. Further, there were, it is argued, many founders—to whom do we turn, then, as controlling authorities? Surely there were many founders, in one sense: the delegates to the Constitutional Convention; the delegates to the ratifying conventions in the several states; and even the people within the several states who wrote and printed and argued endlessly over the Constitution. The key here is not that my Madison is somehow better than your Hamilton or your Thomas Jefferson better than my Richard Henry Lee. The issue, rather, is the common ground that generation shared. And there was much common ground. Even among the leading Federalists and Anti-Federalists, as Herbert Storing has shown, there was much agreement.[13] Indeed, few understood better what the intentions behind the various provisions of the Constitution were than the Anti-Federalist critics, and much can be gleaned from them even though they lost the big battle. Further, does anyone seriously doubt that some framers are better than others in revealing what lies behind the words of the Constitution? Isn't it fair to say that a Madison is a better source of knowledge on most matters than, say, a Nathaniel Gorham? Or that George Mason is a more trustworthy guide than, say, Nicholas Gilman? Surely it is safe to say and easy to prove that some founders are more reliable than others in exposing that all-important common ground of republicanism on which their generation stood.[14]

Third, it is often heard that a jurisprudence of original intention is to be rejected because it ignores all American history since 1787. Justices John Paul Stevens and Thurgood Marshall have most recently offered this bit of questionable insight.[15] The fact is that no one who argues for a jurisprudence of original intention has suggested that somehow all subsequent amendments should be ignored. Amendments are, after all, parts of the Constitution. Thus a jurisprudence of original intention at a minimum demands that every part of the Constitution added since 1787 be accorded the same respect as the original unamended text. This is, to say the least, the oddest and the weakest of the arguments that are usually made against an original intent approach: it is at best a vehement denial by its critics of a proposition that has never been suggested by its friends.

Fourth and finally, the critics of the original intention approach to constitutional interpretation allege that it was never the "original intention" of the framers that "original intention" be the guide to constitutional construction.[16] I will pass over the obvious logical problem of how those who deny the possibility of knowing original intention can thus claim that it was part of the original intention not to use original intention. It is enough to listen to that generation of founders directly. As Madison said in the 1820s:

> if the sense in which the Constitution was accepted and ratified by the nation . . . be not the guide in expounding it, there can be no security for a consistent and stable, more than for a faithful, exercise of its powers. If the meaning of the text be sought in the changeable meaning of the words composing it, it is evident that the shape and attributes of the Government must partake of the changes to which the words and phrases of all living languages are constantly subject. What a metamorphosis would be produced in the code of law if all its ancient phraseology were to be taken in its modern sense![17]

A New Constitutionalism

Ultimately the motive of the critics of a jurisprudence of original intention is not political philosophy and history in the traditional sense; it is ordinary partisan politics and ideology in the contemporary sense. Over the past quarter-century or so, the federal judiciary generally and the Supreme Court in particular have come to engage ever more blatantly in policy making, in foisting upon the more representative institutions at both the national and state levels, and hence upon the people of the nation, a certain ideological view of how the political world ought to be.

The courts have proved to be a much more certain path to this liberal promised land than Congress or the state houses. Influenced

5

by the articles and arguments of those whom Walter Dellinger of Duke Law School has admiringly described as "particularly ingenious scholars," the courts have created new doctrines and new rights that have no connection with the text of the Constitution or the intentions of those who wrote, proposed, and ratified that text.[18] As a result, we have come to see a very strange phenomenon emerge from the legal, academic, and judicial communities; it is a constitutionalism bereft of the Constitution.

This new view of the Constitution, this aconstitutional constitutionalism, seeks to supplement and, if necessary, supplant the written Constitution of 1787 with contemporary notions of higher law; its intellectual project is to infuse constitutional law with contemporary moral theory. In the place of the text and intention of the written Constitution has come what Justice William Brennan has called an evolving conception of human dignity that should, he says, guide our judges as they construe the Constitution.[19] The implicit ideological goal of the new constitutionalism is equally simple. Under this new scheme original intention is to be replaced by judicial pretension. The Constitution is reduced to constitutional law, and popular government is thereby reduced to government by judiciary. A jurisprudence of original intention inevitably frustrates the political and ideological goals of such moral judicial activists.[20]

The result of this new understanding is not limited government in any meaningful sense; surely it is not constitutional government in the most important sense. This new jurisprudence turns a blind eye to the dangers of governmental power by forgetting that judicial power is still fundamentally governmental power—regardless of how benevolent or ideologically pleasing it may appear to some. Such confidence in the courts to wield their awesome powers in the name of moral progress forgets—tragically forgets—what Philip B. Kurland once called the "derelicts of constitutional law," such cases as *Dred Scott* v. *Sandford* (1857), *Plessy* v. *Ferguson* (1896), *Lochner* v. *New York* (1905), and, one must say, *Griswold* v. *Connecticut* (1965) and *Roe* v. *Wade* (1973). To argue for allowing judges to approach the cases and controversies that come before them as moral problems to which they are duty bound to find solutions is to risk allowing the judges (as Chancellor James Kent once said) "to roam at large in the trackless fields of their own imaginations."[21]

In the political sense, this is the legacy of the Supreme Court under Chief Justice Earl Warren. In a famous article in the *Harvard Law Review* in 1971, Judge J. Skelly Wright derided those whom he characterized as "self-appointed scholastic mandarins," those scholars—such as Kurland and Alexander M. Bickel—who had come to criticize the Warren Court's unprincipled activism.[22] To Judge Wright

6

these professors were missing the deeper point of the Warren Court revolution. There was no doubt that the Warren Court was transforming American politics and society, but that would not be its greatest legacy. The true importance of the Warren Court, said Wright, was the revolutionary influence it was having on the thinking of a generation of law students. The Warren Court was teaching that generation that there need be no gulf between law and morality; it was teaching them to recite the language of idealism.

That generation of morally inspired law students has now produced many of our judges and leading professors of law. Guided unswervingly by what Kurland once termed the "egalitarian ethos," this new generation has undertaken to do what it sees as justice, often ignoring such longstanding and textually rooted principles as federalism and separation of powers.[23] The result has not been public beneficence; it has only been judicial aggrandizement at the expense of the other institutional arrangements wisely provided by the Constitution.

Where for generations the Constitution was understood as the embodiment of a fundamental law anchored in clearly discernible political principles, today the Constitution is thought of by these new constitutional moralists as little more than an "old bottle" into which each age legitimately pours its "new wine."[24] This notion of a living Constitution denies that there is any fundamental meaning to the Constitution whereby our politics must be guided. It accepts quite the opposite view, that judges should redefine the meaning of the Constitution according to their own "fresh moral insight."[25]

The contemporary appeal to moral philosophy as a guide to constitutional construction is not, however, an appeal to natural law or higher law in any traditional sense. It is not the understanding of higher law to which such men as Thomas Jefferson, John Marshall, Joseph Story, and Abraham Lincoln on occasion appealed. The new higher law constitutionalism is not an effort aimed at the explication of natural law in some antecedent sense, a body of law that had come to be revealed over time through human experience as a close approximation to justice.[26] Rather, the new mode is forward looking; it is, in the final analysis, not experiential but existential.[27] The new role of political philosophy in constitutional construction is not as a tradition to which judges appeal—to, say, John Locke on property or Montesquieu on separation of powers—but as an activity in which judges themselves must actively engage. Moral theory becomes constitutional praxis.[28]

The result of the Warren Court's revolution in law and its effort to effect "a fusion of constitutional law and moral theory"[29] has been a new and troubling "political jurisprudence"; Warren's own belief that

7

his appointment was a "mission to do justice" subsequently inspired a growing number of other judges that they, too, possessed "roving commissions to do good."[30] Constitutional rights and powers in the traditional sense are no longer simply the point. The task of the judge has become "to give meaning to constitutional values . . . by working within the constitutional text, history, and social ideals. He searches for what is true, right, and just."[31]

Ronald Dworkin's view that courts "should work out principles of legality, equality, and the rest, revise those principles from time to time in the light of what seems to the Court fresh moral insight, and judge the acts of Congress, the states, and the president accordingly" reveals, in a very basic way, the core of the contemporary jurisprudential view. The courts must be willing to take the "vague" terms of the Constitution and give them sound meaning; they must be willing, Dworkin has argued, "to frame and answer questions of political morality."[32] As another contemporary writer has put it:

> The Constitution is an intentionally incomplete, often deliberately indeterminate structure for the participatory evolution of political ideals and governmental practices. . . . The best we can hope for is to encourage wise reflection—through strict scrutiny of any government action or deliberate omission that appears to transgress what it means to be human at a given time and place.[33]

When judges undertake (as they must according to this school of thought) to fill the "gaping holes" in the Constitution's meaning, it must be with "a substantive vision of the needs of the human personality." Neither the text nor the intention of the Constitution can be expected to serve as a guide for this moral adjudication. Rather, it is "the social context of asserted rights" that ultimately is "crucial to the formation of 'substantive judgment' the judges are called upon to exercise."[34] What are to be invoked and appealed to are judicially defined public values that are understood as making up the "moral ambience of the social world we can only inhabit together."[35]

There is no confusion about where these public values are to come from; they will emerge from the judges' "own moral vision," from their "own values." This is not to be merely a case of judges "invoking established moral conventions." Far from it. Under this new jurisprudential order the judges are expected to resolve "moral problems not simply by looking backward to the sediment of old moralities, but ahead to emergent principles in terms of which fragments of a new moral order can be forged."[36] Thus the new goal of judicial review is not merely securing constitutional or legal rights; its goal now is nothing less than the "moral evolution" of the nation.[37]

8

At its deepest level the new constitutionalism seeks to clear a judicial path around and behind the Constitution to what one writer has termed the *"ethos* of the American polity." To be morally significant, judicial review must appeal to that ethos in order to deduce constitutional values and rules "whether they are embodied in the text [of the Constitution] or not."[38] The object is the judicial creation of new "nontextual" rights.[39] The basic premise of this school of juridical thinking is simply that the Constitution left in judicial hands "the considerable power to define and enforce fundamental rights without substantial guidance from constitutional text and history."[40] Thomas Grey has expressed this view most clearly:

> For the generation that framed the Constitution the concept of a "higher law," protecting "natural rights," and taking precedence over ordinary positive law as a matter of political obligation, was widely shared and deeply felt. An essential element of American constitutionalism was the reduction to written form—and hence to positive law—of some of the principles of natural rights. But at the same time, it was generally recognized that written constitutions could not completely codify the higher law. Thus in the framing of the original American constitutions it was widely accepted that there remained unwritten but still binding principles of higher law. The Ninth Amendment is the textual expression of this idea in the Federal Constitution.
>
> As it came to be accepted that the judiciary had the power to enforce the commands of the written Constitution when these conflicted with ordinary law, it was also widely assumed that judges should enforce as constitutional restraints the unwritten natural rights as well.[41]

Nowhere is this new jurisprudential approach better seen than in the arguments that still swirl about the 1965 case of *Griswold* v. *Connecticut,* in which the Supreme Court invalidated a Connecticut statute that prohibited the dissemination of birth control information and devices even to married couples.[42] The Court invalidated that state law on the grounds that it violated the Constitution's right to privacy. What made the case so controversial then—and why it remains controversial today—is that the Constitution does not speak of a right to privacy; the Court simply created one.

Judicially Created Rights

Griswold v. *Connecticut* stands, along with *Dred Scott* v. *Sandford* (1857)[43] and *Lochner* v. *New York* (1905),[44] as one of the "derelicts" of constitutional law because, like *Dred Scott* and *Lochner, Griswold* was a gross and unprincipled expansion of judicial power at the expense of popular government. As in *Dred Scott* and *Lochner,* the Court in *Griswold* preempted the right of the people to make moral judgments as to how their public lives should be governed.

In *Dred Scott* the Court invalidated a national effort to curtail the expansion of slavery into the territories and went beyond that to declare that blacks were not and could not be deemed citizens under the Constitution—regardless of what Congress wished to do. There was no clear constitutional warrant for this decision. It was the first appearance of the idea of substantive due process by which the Court expanded the meaning of liberty in that clause to mean what the judges wanted it to mean.[45] In the *Dred Scott* case, that meant the protection of the slaveholder's vested right of property—his slave.

In *Lochner* the Court invalidated an effort by the legislature of New York to promote the general welfare by regulating the hours bakers could work. This exercise of the traditional police powers formerly understood to be reserved to the states by the Constitution was struck down because it violated something called the "liberty of contract," the then current example of substantive due process. Again, the Court saw fit to preempt the political process and the popular impulse to do what the people thought was right—on no firmer basis than an extratextual, judicially created constitutional doctrine.

The Court in *Griswold* did precisely the same thing. Disagreeing with the law in question—a law Justice Potter Stewart in his dissent referred to as an "uncommonly silly law"—the Court sought some constitutional ground for striking it down.[46] As C. Herman Pritchett has said, when the Court realized it could find no such ground, it created one, "just as it had done with Substantive Due Process three quarters of a century earlier."[47]

In the majority opinion by Justice William O. Douglas, the Court held that a "zone of privacy" existed within the Constitution. This zone was not textually explicit but was, rather, the result of judicial creativity. Justice Douglas found this new and general right to privacy in the fact that "specific guarantees in the Bill of Rights have penumbras, formed by emanations from those guarantees that help give them life and substance." The present case, he concluded, "concerns a relationship lying within the zone of privacy created by several fundamental constitutional guarantees." The reason, to Douglas, seemed clear. "We deal," he said, "with a right of privacy older than the Bill of Rights—older than our political parties, older than our school system." To Douglas this right of marital privacy was so fundamental that it simply had to be in the Constitution somewhere. When he could not find it, he simply put it there.[48]

However troubling was Justice Douglas's opinion, the real travesty of *Griswold* is to be found in the concurring opinion by Justice Arthur J. Goldberg.[49] For in that opinion not only did Justice Goldberg "rediscover" the Ninth Amendment, he totally rewrote it by distorting the history and the intention that underlay it. One would be hard pressed to think of a more intellectually dishonest opinion than Justice Goldberg's in *Griswold*—unless one remembers that of Justice Roger Taney in *Dred Scott* or that of Justice Rufus Peckham in *Lochner.* The constitutional historian Alfred H. Kelly said at the time that Justice Goldberg's concurrence, with its "astonishing resuscitation of the Ninth Amendment," was a "curious mixture of law-office history and vaulting legal logic." Such a use of history by the Court as a "precedent-breaking device" to get rid of laws the justices do not agree with, Kelly noted, is nothing less than "a Marxist-type perversion of the relation between truth and utility. It assumes that history can be written to serve the interests of libertarian idealism." Allowing such distorted history to "run wild in judicial opinions," Kelly concluded, can have "disastrous" consequences.[50]

Justice Goldberg's law-office history was precise. "The language and history of the Ninth Amendment," he argued, "reveal that the Framers of the Constitution believed that there are additional fundamental rights, protected from governmental infringement, which exist alongside those fundamental rights specifically mentioned in the first eight constitutional amendments. . . . To hold that a right so basic and so deep-rooted in our society as the right to privacy in marriage may be infringed because that right is not guaranteed in so many words by the first eight amendments . . . is to ignore the Ninth Amendment and to give it no effect whatsoever."[51]

Goldberg was careful to try and hedge his activist bets:

> In determining which rights are fundamental, judges are not left at large to decide cases in light of their personal and private notions. Rather, they must look to the "traditions and [collective] conscience of our people" to determine whether a principle is "so rooted [there] as to be ranked as fundamental."[52]

This was not, however, so tough a task, he concluded:

> Although the Constitution does not speak in so many words of the right of privacy in marriage, I cannot believe that it offers those fundamental rights no protection. . . . I believe

that the right of privacy in the marital relation is fundamental and basic—a personal right within the meaning of the Ninth Amendment.[53]

The fact is, however, that what one believes is a matter of "personal and private notions" unless one can make a convincing case that such a notion is rooted in a more general principle, that it has some origin in the text of the Constitution or in the intentions of those who wrote, proposed, and ratified that text.[54] The arbitrary nature of Justice Goldberg's logic is revealed by his confession that the statutes of Connecticut that made it illegal to engage in adultery or fornication out of wedlock were "beyond doubt" constitutional. One has to ask why that should be so. If a right of privacy is so fundamental as to be constitutionally protected, surely it must attach more to the individual as an individual than to any relationship that individual might find himself in at any given moment. Surely adultery and fornication—not to mention homosexual sodomy and bestiality—are matters of privacy considered as an individual right. The fact is that statutes governing such activities did not offend the judicial sensibilities in the way statutes governing contraceptive use by married couples did. What this means is that the constitutional standard being employed is inherently arbitrary and capricious; it depends not on the Constitution but only on the moral mood of the Court.[55]

The arbitrariness of the constitutional standard employed by Justice Goldberg is not the deepest problem. The real problem with his opinion is its blatant rewriting of history. The fact is that the Ninth Amendment no less than the nine other provisions of the Bill of Rights must be read in light of the intentions that prompted its passage. When that is done, there is no way one can accept Goldberg's thesis concerning that amendment's "language and history"; to assert, as Justice Goldberg did in *Griswold*, that the Ninth Amendment is some sort of metaphysical trapdoor to a world of constitutionally undefined but nonetheless constitutionally protected rights waiting to be discovered and invoked by the Court against the states is, as Justice Stewart said in his scathing dissent in that case, to turn "somersaults with history." It shows well how dangerous is a judicial disregard for original intention.[56]

The truth of the matter is that the Bill of Rights was proposed and ratified at the demand of the critics of the Constitution of 1787, the Anti-Federalists. The Anti-Federalists—whose ranks included some of the most preeminent public men of that time, such as Patrick Henry, George Mason, and Richard Henry Lee—feared the new and untested national government created by the Constitution. They viewed the states as the primary guarantors of their freedoms and the new and powerful national government as a threat to that system. At a minimum, they argued, the new government should be shackled by a declaration of fundamental rights, a staking out of the areas into which the new government could not go.

One of the primary concerns of the Anti-Federalists was the maintenance of the federal order rooted in the idea of a national government of limited and enumerated powers resting upon a collection of states that were still very sovereign even though not completely so. Although Roger Sherman in the federal convention assured a worried George Mason that the new Constitution would in no way repeal the existing state declarations of rights, the Anti-Federalists remained skeptical. As Patrick Henry put it in the Virginia ratifying convention, "A general positive provision should be inserted in the new system, securing to the States and the people every right which was not conceded to the general government."[57] This concern was met by the Ninth and Tenth amendments, which reserve to the states and the people other rights and other powers, respectively, not clearly preempted by the national Constitution.

The Ninth Amendment had a "specific function, well-understood at the time of its adoption: the maintenance of rights guaranteed by the laws of the States. . . . The retained rights envisioned by the Framers . . . included not only those established by common law and statute as of the Constitution's adoption, but also those to be subsequently established by state legislation. . . . Unenumerated rights were not federal rights, as were the enumerated rights," but were state rights that had not been singled out from the state bills of rights for inclusion in the new, national Bill of Rights. The "Anti-Federalists wished to avoid the possibility that other rights under State law would be rendered a nullity under the proposed Constitution, and therefore sought to obtain a declaration that defeated such a construction." Such was the original intention of the Ninth Amendment; it was "designed not to circumscribe but to protect the enactments of the States."[58]

Beyond confusing the specific constitutional purpose of the Ninth Amendment, Goldberg was also wrong about the substantive nature of the rights left unenumerated by the Ninth Amendment. In particular, "privacy as an all encompassing constitutional right was . . . not a part of the legal tradition inherited from England by the Colonies which would have been secured in either a state or federal bill of rights."[59] The fact is that Justice Goldberg's theory of the Ninth Amendment sprang only from his own imagination; it is one of the clearest examples of the ideological wish being father to the judicial thought.[60]

Beyond the substantive concerns raised by Justice Goldberg's novel theory is a very important question about the legitimate nature and extent of judicial power in dealing with the Ninth Amendment. It is a question that is raised by reflection on another of the Anti-Federalist's primary concerns: the danger of arbitrary judicial power.

The main concern of the Anti-Federalists was probably best captured by the New Yorker Brutus.[61] Brutus pointed out that, in effect, the Constitution, by not specifically tying the judges to the text but allowing them, by implication, to "explain the Constitution according to the reasoning spirit of it, without being confined to the words or letter," granted these unelected and life-tenured officials the power "to mould the government into almost any shape they pleased." In particular, Brutus said, the new and awesome judicial power would move silently and imperceptibly toward completing the tendency of the proposed Constitution, which he saw as the "entire subversion of the legislative, executive, and judicial powers of the individual States."[62]

Brutus's Anti-Federalist colleague the Federal Farmer argued along similar lines. He pointed out that his countrymen were "more in the danger of sowing the seeds of arbitrary government in [the judicial] department than in any other." The reason, the Federal Farmer concluded, was that the grant of judicial power came dangerously close to positing "an arbitrary power of discretion in the judges, to decide as their conscience, their opinions, their caprice, or their politics" might dictate.[63] Such arbitrariness was at odds with constitutional government.

For these reasons alone it is utterly inconceivable that the Ninth Amendment can be properly construed as providing an unchecked grant of power to the Court to create new rights through which the national judiciary can proscribe the domestic policies of the states.

These lessons of the past were not lost on the dissenters in *Griswold*, Justices Hugo Black and Potter Stewart. Black, especially, had long been a foe of his brethren who would seek to smuggle natural law notions into the Constitution by what Madison once derided as "the license of construction."[64] In a famous dissent in *Adamson v. California*, Black had pointed out that "to pass upon the constitutionality of statutes by looking to the particular standards enumerated in the Bill of Rights and other parts of the Constitution is one thing; to invalidate statutes because of application of 'natural law' deemed to be above and undefined by the Constitution is another."[65] Black was not fooled by the "rhapsodical strains" of the arguments of the majority in *Griswold*, either; they were "merely using different words to claim for this Court and for the federal judiciary power to invalidate any legislative act which the judges find irrational, unreasonable or offensive."[66] By any other name the standard the Court would have to use—be it "fairness and justice," "rational purpose," or "the traditions and conscience of our people"—would boil down to one thing and one thing only: "natural justice."[67]

While he, like Stewart, found the law in question both silly and offensive, that did not mean it was also unconstitutional; unconstitutionality had to rest on something more substantial than the Court's judgment of what was wise or necessary.

> I do not believe that we are granted power by the Due Process Clause or any other constitutional provision or provisions to measure constitutionality by our belief that legislation is arbitrary, capricious or unreasonable, or accomplishes no justifiable purpose, or is offensive to our own notions of "civilized standards of conduct." Such an appraisal of the wisdom of legislation is an attribute of the power to make laws, not the power to interpret them.[68]

Further, and more to the point, Black said,

> If any broad, unlimited power to hold laws unconstitutional because they offend what this Court conceives to be the "[collective] conscience of our people" is vested in this Court by the Ninth Amendment, the Fourteenth Amendment, or any other provision of the Constitution, it was not given by the Framers, but rather has been bestowed on the Court by the Court.[69]

When it came to the Ninth Amendment in particular, Black argued, that amendment

> was enacted to protect State powers against federal invasion . . . [not] as a weapon of federal power to prevent State legislatures from passing laws they consider appropriate to govern local affairs. Use of any such broad, unbounded judicial authority would make [the Supreme] Court [into] a day to day constitutional convention.[70]

To allow the Court such a general supervisory power over the states, Black concluded, would amount to "a great unconstitutional shift of power to the courts which . . . will be bad for the courts and worse for the country."[71] In this view Justice Black was echoing the views of the great Justice Oliver Wendell Holmes, who had waged intellectual war against the proponents of the earlier *Lochner* era notions of expansive judicial power. In *Tyson & Brother* v. *Banton* (1927), Holmes had argued in dissent (a dissent the Court eventually

15

took seriously when it overruled *Tyson* only six weeks before *Griswold* in 1965):

> I think the proper course is to recognize that a State legislature can do whatever it sees fit to do unless it is restrained by some express prohibition in the Constitution of the United States or of the State, and that Courts should be careful not to extend such prohibitions beyond their obvious meaning by reading into them conceptions of public policy that the particular court may happen to entertain.[72]

Elsewhere Holmes had argued that he felt "more than anxiety . . . at the ever increasing scope given to the Fourteenth Amendment in cutting down . . . the constitutional rights of the States." It seemed to Holmes that there was "hardly any limit but the sky to the invalidating of those rights if they happen to strike a majority of the Court as for any reason undesirable." Holmes simply rejected out of hand the notion that the Fourteenth Amendment was intended to give the Court "*carte blanche* to embody [its] economic or moral beliefs in its prohibitions." To so construe the Fourteenth Amendment was to commit "to the Court with no guide but the Court's own discretion, the validity of whatever laws the States may pass."[73]

Thinking back to Holmes and those early days of the Court, Black found the majority opinion in *Griswold* indistinguishable from the majority opinion in *Lochner.* And that made *Griswold* as troubling for Black the strict constructionist as *Lochner* had been for Holmes the legal realist. As Black put it:

> I cannot rely on the Due Process Clause or the Ninth Amendment or any mysterious and uncertain natural law concept as a reason for striking down this state law. The Due Process Clause with an "arbitrary and capricious," or "shocking to the conscience" formula was liberally used by this Court to strike down economic legislation in the early decades of this century, threatening, many people thought, the tranquility and stability of the nation. See, e.g. *Lochner* v. *New York,* 198 U.S. 45. That formula, based on subjective considerations of "natural justice," is no less dangerous when used to enforce this Court's views about personal rights than those about economic rights.[74]

For Black, as for Holmes, the Court's reliance on "natural law due process philosophy" to strike down legislation was simply unacceptable. As Learned Hand had once pointed out, all the highfalutin rhetoric could not hide the fact that such decisions rested on nothing more elevated than the judges' "personal preferences." For a judge to exercise judicial review as a means of allegedly giving meaning to "inscrutable principles" was to assume himself properly a "communal mentor" whose every decision had a kind of " 'moral radiation' " about it; this struck Judge Hand as "a very dubious addition" to any judge's powers.[75] It struck Black exactly the same way.[76]

Conclusion

In the final analysis the problem with the majority opinions in *Griswold* v. *Connecticut* is their willingness to confuse the question of what is just with the question of what is constitutional. It is precisely this same confusion that renders contemporary constitutional theory such a formidable danger to the *idea* of a written Constitution; such theory turns a blind eye to the political consequences of a constitutionalism bereft of the Constitution. It assumes that those who fill the bench will know, in some strict sense, the difference between justice and their mere perception of justice; such an assumption denies that judges, no less than anyone else, are prone to the infirmities of the human condition. Ultimately, the new constitutional jurisprudence rests on blind faith that those who judge will indeed possess a "special kind of substantive rationality" and will be "committed to the notion of moral evolution and . . . themselves open to the possibility of moral growth."[77] Such confidence is a danger to constitutional liberty.[78]

Against this view of constitutional theory is the older view of the founders, the idea that interpretation must be rooted in the text and the original intention behind that text. As Joseph Story put it, the

> fundamental maxim . . . in the interpretation of . . . positive laws is that the intention . . . is to be followed. This intention is to be gathered from the words, the context, the subject matter, the effects and consequences, and the spirit and reason are to be ascertained, not from vague conjecture, but from the motives and language apparent on the face of the law.[79]

While this view may be more morally modest than the current view, it is also safer constitutionally and politically. For at bottom it accepts a basic truth of American constitutionalism. As James Wilson said at the federal convention, "laws may be unwise, may be dangerous, may be destructive . . . and yet not be unconstitutional."[80] This older view of the Constitution—the Constitution understood as positive law—was premised on a belief that when it came to interpreting the Constitution, there were limits to "the Laws of Nature and of Nature's God."

17

Where the Constitution intends to protect rights, it does so—clearly and simply. Where it is silent, it is silent. The due process clauses are not judicial wild cards whereby contemporary moral, political, or economic theories may be made to trump the Constitution's original meaning; the Ninth Amendment is not a statement of unenumerated rights so fundamental and sweeping as to render all the other rights explicitly mentioned in the text superfluous; most of all, Article III is not the primary means whereby rights are to find their primary protection. It would have struck the founders as bizarre to have expected the security of their rights to depend on a judiciary willing to plunge into a moral discourse unattached to the text and divorced from the intentions that lie behind the document itself.

A jurisprudence of original intention appreciates the design and objects of the Constitution. It recognizes the limitations of popular government—such as majority tyranny—and the need to secure individual rights. But it denies that good government and the sound security of rights are ever to be expected from any body of men even if (or especially if) dedicated to the pursuit of higher law. The Constitution with its carefully contrived institutional balances and checks was devised precisely to supply, as Madison said in *Federalist* No. 51, "the defect of better motives."[81] Sturdy institutions replaced good intentions as the source of good government. To allow the courts to enter the realm of substantive policy making is to deny the logic and the limits of the written Constitution. To distrust the moral impulses of judges is not to be morally cynical; it is, rather, to be politically prudent.

The only way the inherently undemocratic power of judicial review can be reconciled with our republican form of government is by keeping it tied to the written Constitution. Only by conforming to the intentions of the people as expressed in the document can the judges legitimate what they do; as they range further from text and intention, their power becomes increasingly illegitimate.

This is the essential dilemma posed by judicial activism. Not only does such activism violate the separation of powers and make judges policy makers at a given moment, but over time it weakens the role of the Court by undermining its only claim to legitimacy—that it is only enforcing the clear will of the people as expressed in their Constitution.

In a democratic republic such as ours, this is a weighty matter. Alexis de Tocqueville in *Democracy in America* noted that the Court rules only by virtue of its moral force in society. Politically, the Court is largely powerless. Its decrees and judgments are given effect only by the deference of the other more powerful branches and ultimately by the deference of the people. Such deference is possible only when the Court can give an accounting of its actions by pointing to a textual reason for its decisions. Thus to argue for a proper attachment of the Court to the Constitution through a jurisprudence of original intention is to argue for judicial power, not against it; it is to argue for nothing less than the idea of the rule of law over the politics of the moment.

Notes

1. Max Farrand, ed., *The Records of the Federal Convention*, 4 vols. (New Haven, Conn.: Yale University Press, 1938), vol. 1, pp. 422, 462; vol. 2, pp. 126, 361. See also *The Federalist*, ed. Jacob Cooke (Middletown, Conn.: Weslyan University Press, 1961), Nos. 14, 37, 53, 63, 78.

2. *Federalist* No. 1, p. 3; No. 6, p. 35; No. 51, p. 349. As Joseph Story pointed out, constitutions "are instruments of a practical nature, founded on the common business of human life, adapted to common wants, designed for common use, and fitted for common understandings." Joseph Story, *Commentaries on the Constitution of the United States*, 2 vols., 3d ed. (Boston: Little, Brown, 1858), vol. 1, p. 322.

See also James Iredell's charge to the grand jury of May 23, 1796: "Liberty without law is anarchy; law without liberty is oppression. A due mixture of both can alone make any people at once prosperous and happy." Griffith J. McRee, ed., *Life and Correspondence of James Iredell*, 2 vols. (New York: D. Appleton and Co., 1857), vol. 2, pp. 483–84.

3. *Federalist* No. 78, p. 525.

4. Ibid.

5. *Federalist* No. 9, p. 51.

6. *Federalist* No. 39, p. 257; No. 51, p. 351.

7. *Federalist* No. 51, p. 347.

8. Speech before the Federalist Society, Northwestern University School of Law, Chicago, Illinois, 1986.

9. Farrand, *Records*, vol. 1, p. 50 (Madison); *Federalist* No. 10, p. 62.

10. Herbert J. Storing, "The Constitution and the Bill of Rights," in M. Judd Harmon, ed., *Essays on the Constitution of the United States* (Port Washington, N.Y.: Kennikat Press, 1978), p. 48.

11. Charles McC. Mathias, Jr., Speech at Clemson University, Clemson, South Carolina, July 12, 1987.

12. See Stanley Elkins and Eric McKitrick, "The Founding Fathers: Young Men of the Revolution," *Political Science Quarterly*, vol. 76, no. 2 (June 1961), pp. 181–216.

13. Herbert J. Storing, *What the Anti-Federalists Were For* (Chicago: University of Chicago Press, 1981).

14. "Contemporary construction," said Story, "is properly resorted to, to illustrate and confirm the text, to explain a doubtful phrase, or to expound an obscure clause; and in proportion to the uniformity and universality of that

construction, and the known ability and talents of those, by whom it was given, is the credit to which it is entitled." *Commentaries,* vol. 1, p. 288.

15. Justice Stevens's speech is reprinted in *U.C. Davis Law Review,* vol. 19 (1985), p. 15.

16. H. Jefferson Powell, "The Original Understanding of Original Intent," *Harvard Law Review,* vol. 98 (1985), p. 885. See also H. Jefferson Powell, "Rules for Originalists," *Virginia Law Review,* vol. 73 (1987), p. 659.

17. James Madison to Henry Lee, June 25, 1824, *Letters and Other Writings of James Madison,* Congressional Ed., 4 vols. (Philadelphia: J. B. Lippincott and Co., 1865), vol. 3, pp. 441–43.

18. Walter Dellinger, remarks at the Smithsonian Institution Bicentennial Symposium on "The Constitution: Roots, Rights, and Responsibilities," Charlottesville, Virginia, and Washington, D.C., May 10–22, 1987.

In thinking of these "ingenious" scholars, one is reminded of Edward S. Corwin's apt quip that "if judges make law, so do commentators," and of Jefferson, who once described Thomas Paine as a man "who thought more than he read." Edward S. Corwin, "Review: *The Law of the American Constitution,* by Charles K. Burdick," *Michigan Law Review,* vol. 22 (November 1923), p. 84. Thomas Jefferson to Major John Cartwright, June 5, 1824, *The Writings of Thomas Jefferson,* ed. Andrew Lipscomb, 20 vols. (Washington, D.C.: Thomas Jefferson Memorial Foundation, 1905), vol. 16, p. 43.

19. William J. Brennan, Jr., "The Constitution of the United States: Contemporary Ratification," reprinted in *U.C. Davis Law Review,* vol. 19 (1985), p. 2.

20. See Mark Tushnet, "The Sociology of Article III," *Harvard Law Review,* vol. 93 (1979), p. 1698; and Owen Fiss, "The Social and Political Foundations of Adjudication," in Robert A. Goldwin and William A. Schambra, eds., *How Does the Constitution Secure Rights?* (Washington, D.C.: American Enterprise Institute, 1985).

21. James Kent, *Commentaries on American Law,* 4 vols. (New York: O. Halsted, 1826), vol. 1, p. 321.

22. J. Skelly Wright, "Professor Bickel, the Scholarly Tradition, and the Supreme Court," *Harvard Law Review,* vol. 84 (1971), pp. 769, 777.

23. Philip B. Kurland, *Politics, the Constitution, and the Warren Court* (Chicago: University of Chicago Press, 1970), p. xx.

24. John Roche, "Judicial Self-Restraint," *American Political Science Review,* vol. 49 (1955), pp. 762, 763.

25. Ronald Dworkin, *Taking Rights Seriously* (Cambridge, Mass.: Harvard University Press, 1977), p. 137.

26. As Joseph Story described it, law was "founded not upon any will, but upon the discovery of a right already existing, which is to be drawn either from the internal legislation of human reason, or the historical development of the nation." Joseph Story, "Law, Legislation, and Codes," reprinted in James McClellan, *Joseph Story and the American Constitution* (Norman: University of Oklahoma Press, 1971), p. 365.

27. Consider Leo Strauss: "Traditional natural law is primarily and mainly an objective 'rule and measure,' a binding order prior to, and independent of

the human will, while modern natural law tends to be primarily and mainly a series of 'rights,' of subjective claims originating in the human will." Leo Strauss, *The Political Philosophy of Hobbes* (Chicago: University of Chicago Press, 1939), pp. xi–xii.

28. One such writer has put it this way: "Besides using text, structure, and precedent, a justice considering what rights Americans have may turn to our political traditions and to moral philosophy. . . . By fusing constitutional interpretation and moral theory, principled activism vindicates the Constitution's authority by establishing its rightness. . . . By engaging in moral reflection rather than historical researches to complete the Constitution's difficult passages, judges help justify and vindicate the Constitution's moral supremacy [and] help realize the Constitution's moral aspirations. . . . The Ninth Amendment [for example] calls upon conscientious interpreters to reflect on natural rights and to engage in moral theory." Stephen Macedo, *The New Right v. The Constitution* (Washington, D.C.: Cato Institute, 1986), pp. 4, 8, 12–13, 38–39.

29. Dworkin, *Taking Rights Seriously,* p. 149.

30. Martin Shapiro, "Judge as Statesman, Judge as Pol," *New York Times,* November 21, 1981, Book Review Section, p. 42; G. Edward White, *Earl Warren: A Public Life* (New York: Oxford University Press, 1982), pp. 350–69; and Alexander M. Bickel, *The Supreme Court and the Idea of Progress* (New York: Harper and Row, 1970), p. 134.

31. Owen Fiss, "The Forms of Justice," *Harvard Law Review,* vol. 93 (1979), pp. 1, 9.

32. Dworkin, *Taking Rights Seriously,* p. 147.

33. Laurence Tribe, *American Constitutional Law* (Mineola, N.Y.: Foundation Press, 1978), pp. iii, 892.

34. Ibid., pp. 889, 891.

35. Frank Michelman, "Politics and Values or What's Really Wrong with Rationality Review?" *Creighton Law Review,* vol. 13 (1979), pp. 487, 502.

36. Michael Perry, *The Constitution, the Court, and Human Rights* (New Haven, Conn.: Yale University Press, 1980), pp. 123, 125, 101, 111, 99.

37. Ibid., p. 101.

38. Philip Bobbitt, *Constitutional Fate* (New York: Oxford University Press, 1982), pp. 94, 125.

39. Ibid., p. 143.

40. Thomas Grey, "Do We Have an Unwritten Constitution?" *Stanford Law Review,* vol. 27 (1975), pp. 703, 714.

41. Ibid., pp. 715–16.

42. 381 U.S. 479 (1965).

43. 19 Howard 393 (1857).

44. 198 U.S. 45 (1905).

45. As Corwin noted, with *Dred Scott,* "Due Process of Law came . . . to mean the Court's idea of what was just." "The Dissolving Structure of Our Constitutional Law," *Presidential Power and the Constitution: Essays by Edward S. Corwin,* ed. Richard Loss (Ithaca, N.Y.: Cornell University Press, 1976), p. 154.

46. 381 U.S. 479, 527.

47. C. Herman Pritchett, *The American Constitution*, 2d ed. (Chicago: Rand McNally, 1968), p. 686.

48. 381 U.S. 479, 484–86. See Robert H. Bork, "Neutral Principles and Some First Amendment Problems," *Indiana Law Journal*, vol. 47 (1971), p. 1. The year after *Griswold* Douglas would go even further in dealing with the equal protection clause: "The Equal Protection Clause is not shackled to the political theory of a particular era. In determining what lines are unconstitutionally discriminatory, we have never been confined to historic notions of equality any more than we have restricted due process to a fixed catalogue of what was at a given time deemed to be the limits of fundamental rights. Notions of what constitute equal treatment for purposes of the Equal Protection Clause *do* change." Harper v. Virginia Board of Elections, 383 U.S. 663 (1966), 699.

49. The significance of the Goldberg concurrence does not lie in its power as a dominant rule of construction today; there has yet to be any statute invalidated under the Ninth Amendment. The significance of Goldberg's opinion lies in what history is likely to prove to be its pivotal role as the beginning of the next dominant wave of judicial activism based on natural law.

50. Alfred H. Kelly, "Clio and the Court: An Illicit Love Affair," in Philip B. Kurland, ed., *The Supreme Court Review: 1965* (Chicago: University of Chicago Press, 1966), pp. 150, 155, 157.

51. 381 U.S. 479, at 488, 491.

52. Ibid., at 493.

53. Ibid., at 400.

54. Walter Berns, "Judicial Review and the Rights and Laws of Nature," in Philip B. Kurland et al., eds., *The Supreme Court Review: 1982* (Chicago: University of Chicago Press, 1983), pp. 49–83.

55. See, for example, Bowers v. Hardwick, 106 S. Ct. 2841 (1986).

56. Alfred H. Kelly offered a corrective view of the founders' understanding of natural law. Said Kelly: "Natural law theory, in which Madison and other political leaders of the Revolutionary era were steeped, was a large and expansive notion. But it was not limitless. Ultimately, Revolutionary natural-rights theorists insisted, liberty was derived from a state of nature, but it had long since been given a very positive and specific content. . . . The notion of pulling new natural rights from the air to allow for an indefinite expansion can hardly be considered to be within the original spirit of the [Ninth] Amendment, even if we assume that Madison was attempting a vague guarantee of rights that he did not care to enumerate." "Clio and the Court." pp. 154–55.

57. Sherman and Mason in Farrand, *Records*, vol. 2, p. 588; and Henry in Jonathan Elliot, ed., *Debates in the Several State Ratifying Conventions*, 5 vols. (Philadelphia: J. B. Lippincott and Co., 1876), vol. 3, p. 150.

58. Russell L. Caplan, "The History and Meaning of the Ninth Amendment," *University of Virginia Law Review*, vol. 69 (1983), pp. 223, 227, 248, 259–60, 245. As Raoul Berger has pointed out: "It is incongruous . . . to read the text of the Ninth Amendment as expanding *federal* powers at the very same moment

that the tenth was reserving to the states or to the people all 'powers not delegated' . . . because the federal government may not *'deny'* unenumerated rights, it does not follow that it may *enforce* them against the states." Raoul Berger, "The Ninth Amendment," *Cornell Law Review*, vol. 66 (1980), pp. 1, 8.

59. Ibid., p. 262.

60. Ibid., p. 267. As Kelly has noted, Goldberg's misconstruction of the Ninth Amendment was "little more than a way of returning to an open-ended concept of substantive due process after *Lochner.*" "Clio and the Court," p. 155.

61. See Ann Stuart Diamond, "The Anti-Federalist *Brutus,*" *Political Science Reviewer: 1976.*

62. Letter XI of *Brutus,* January 31, 1788, in Herbert J. Storing, ed., *The Complete Anti-Federalist,* 7 vols. (Chicago: University of Chicago Press, 1981), vol. 2, item 97, par. 137.

63. Letters from the *Federal Farmer,* in Storing, *The Complete Anti-Federalist,* vol. 2, item 8, par. 185; vol. 1, item 8, par. 195; vol. 2, item 8, par. 42.

64. James Madison to Thomas Ritchie, December 18, 1825, in Madison, *Letters and Other Writings,* vol. 3, p. 506.

65. 332 U.S. 46, 92 (1947).

66. 381 U.S. 479, at 511.

67. Ibid.

68. Ibid., at 513.

69. Ibid., at 520.

70. Ibid.

71. Ibid.

72. 273 U.S. 418, 446 (1927).

73. Baldwin v. Missouri, 281 U.S. 586, 595 (1930).

74. 381 U.S. 479, 522.

75. Learned Hand, *The Bill of Rights* (Cambridge, Mass.: Harvard University Press, 1958), pp. 70–71.

76. Justice Stewart was equally appalled by the majority opinion in *Griswold.* "I think this is an uncommonly silly law," he said. "But we are not asked . . . to say whether we think this law is unwise or even asinine. We are asked to hold that it violates the United States Constitution. And that I cannot do." Stewart further pointed out that the Court had been urged during oral argument to strike down the Connecticut law because it did not " 'conform to current community standards.' " This struck Stewart as especially bizarre. "If, as I should surely hope, the law before us does not reflect the standards of the people of Connecticut, the people of Connecticut can freely exercise their true Ninth and Tenth Amendment rights to persuade their elected representatives to repeal it. That is the constitutional way to take this law off the books," at 527, 530, 531.

77. Fiss, "The Forms of Justice," p. 34; and Perry, *The Constitution, the Courts, and Human Rights,* p. 143. Or, as Justice Brennan once confessed, the Court must be willing to abandon the "discredited moral prejudice of bygone centuries." Labine v. Vincent, 401 U.S. 532, 541 (1971).

78. As Justice Louis Brandeis once said, albeit in a different context: "The

greatest dangers to liberty lurk in insidious encroachment by men of zeal, well meaning but without understanding." Olmstead v. United States, 277 U.S. 438, 479 (1928).

79. Story, "Law, Legislation, and Codes," p. 350.
80. Farrand, *Records,* vol. 2, p. 73.
81. *Federalist* No. 51, p. 349.

2

How the Constitution
Establishes Justice

Abram Chayes

What does the Constitution do "to establish justice"? Here is a deceptively simple answer: it provides for "the judicial power of the United States" to be exercised by "one Supreme Court and such other courts as Congress may ordain and establish." In the quasi-constitutional Judiciary Act of 1789, many members of the Constitutional Convention, sitting now as congressmen, rounded out the work by establishing the lower federal courts, which in one form or another have been with us ever since.

The federal judiciary is the institutional custodian of justice in our system. I do not mean by this to denigrate the other departments of government in which the founders vested other powers of the new state. Nor do I mean to say that Congress and the executive are never or ought never to be concerned with justice. But compared with providing for the common defense or promoting the general welfare, establishing justice requires a longer view, responding to values and considerations both less tangible and more transcendent than are commonly emphasized by elected political leaders conducting the ordinary affairs of government. So the judicial department, less responsive to transient political currents and relying, as the framers said, on reason rather than will as its activating principle, is the institutional custodian of justice, just as Congress controls the purse and the president is the institutional embodiment of the nation in war and foreign affairs.

The judicial department established by the framers was unique in 1787, and to a large extent it remains unique today. The Constitution establishes the judiciary as a coequal branch of government, on the same plane as the other two and responsible jointly with them for the governance of the state. No other judicial system can make that statement.

All modern societies have judges, and an independent judiciary is a hallmark of liberal democracy. But outside the United States, judicial systems are regarded primarily as a service provided by the government, much like an educational system or a sewage system, to take care of the workaday business of disposing of the disputes that arise in the ordinary course of social and economic life. They are not partners in the governance of those societies.

In 1787, such a judiciary was a new thing under the sun. Perhaps more than any other innovation of the Constitution, it deserves to be called an invention, although to some extent an inadvertent invention, of the framers.

Eighteenth-century American political thinkers were very familiar with the structure and problems of legislative assemblies and executive organs. The main battles of the previous two centuries of English political life had been fought out between partisans of Parliament and Crown. Locke and Montesquieu, whose guardian spirits, as we are taught, hovered over Independence Hall in Philadelphia, had addressed themselves primarily to the relationship between these two institutions. Locke, of course, was concerned that judges should be independent, so that the king could not dictate results in cases in which he was concerned. The independence of the judiciary in this sense was one of the important achievements of the Act of Settlement. Beyond that, Locke saw the judiciary as part of the law enforcement machinery, and thus in some sense as an extension of the executive.

Montesquieu did define the judiciary as a separate branch of government—perhaps in response to the rule of tripartite division that still dominates French intellectual life. His conception of its role, however, was more meager even than Locke's. The judge was the mouthpiece of the law, nothing more. He was confined to the mechanical task of announcing its consequences in particular cases. Neither Locke nor Montesquieu conceived of the judiciary as having a substantive role in the government of the polity.

It is not quite fair to say that the invention of "the judicial power," in our sense, at the convention was inadvertent. Although the framers' conception of the judiciary did not look much like our contemporary institution, any more than they anticipated the twentieth-century Congress or presidency, their thinking clearly went beyond Locke and Montesquieu.

The most salient feature of the courts as governors is judicial review of legislative action. That power, as we know, is nowhere mentioned in the Constitution (which must give some pause to strict constructionists). But many of the framers saw it as implicit in the conception of government under a written constitution and expected that courts would exercise it as a matter of course. The theory, in essentially the same form it takes in *Marbury* v. *Madison*, is expounded by Hamilton in *The Federalist*, and of course Hamilton did not speak for himself alone.

There is much additional evidence that the framers understood the judicial power as power to govern. Both the Federalists and their opponents in the convention recognized the debates and struggles over the existence of a separate federal court system and the jurisdiction of federal courts to be debates about the power of the federal government and especially the power of the federal government relative to the states.

All agreed that a federal Supreme Court was necessary to safeguard the uniform application of federal law. To create a federal court system below the Supreme Court, however, was to expand the power of the federal government. If all cases were necessarily remitted in the first instance to state courts, of uncertain tenure and subject to local influence, the power of the federal government, its ability to govern and impose its will, would be curbed. If the categories of cases that could be heard in the federal courts were expanded, the power of the states was by that much reduced.

One of the great compromises of the convention concerned just these questions. The resolution was to provide ample power in Article III, both to create federal courts and to vest them with jurisdiction over a wide but defined range of matters of common concern. But the decision about whether and how much was remitted to the Congress.

In practice that turned out to mean the First Congress. There the Federalists were in stronger control than in the convention, and they resolved most of the open issues in their favor. In particular, they established the lower federal courts, a decision that surely had constitutional dimensions. And they made general grants of admiralty and diversity jurisdiction. (When federal questions began to appear with increasing frequency as a result of the Civil War amendments and the dawning age of federal regulation, the Congress responded in like measure with a general grant of federal question jurisdiction.)

The work of the convention in instating the judicial power was complete.

Evolution of the Powers of the Court

How has the judicial branch exercised its power to govern? The usual answer focuses on the distinctive institution of judicial review, emphasizing the adversary relationship between court and legislature

27

and calibrating the level of constraint judges have imposed on legislative bodies at a given period. That line of analysis is important, and we shall return to it, but it deflects attention from the more general lawmaking powers of the federal courts.

Lawmaking Authority. For the first half-century or so, the federal judiciary was a lawmaking authority for the nation at least coequal in importance with the Congress. The national legislature turned its attention to structural matters—a revenue-raising tariff, the monetary system, veterans' pensions, the administration of the virgin lands to the west, the army and navy, and relations with the Indians. Very little of the output of the early congresses addressed relations between private persons in the affairs of everyday life. Indeed, it was not clear that such matters were within the enumerated powers of the national legislature. Even the first permanent federal bankruptcy law was not enacted until 1898, though the bankruptcy power is expressly mandated in Article I.

At the same time, the federal courts were elaborating a relatively uniform body of common law governing large-scale economic transactions, much as Mansfield, a century earlier, had developed a commercial law for the burgeoning activity of English merchants. The admiralty jurisdiction, which was exclusively federal, brought much of America's international commerce within the reach of judge-made law laid down by the federal courts—marine insurance, carriage of goods by sea, collisions, and other such maritime torts.

In the diversity jurisdiction, federal judges went routinely about the business of applying a uniform common law of sales, negotiable instruments, and much more to private transactions and activities concerning more states than one. We are taught to see the root of this heresy in *Swift v. Tyson*, but my guess is that Justice Story only put the stamp of approval on doing what came naturally for federal judges.

Justice Frankfurter, in helping (with gusto) to lay *Swift v. Tyson* to rest, remarked that the opinion reflected a jurisprudence, "a particular way of looking at the law," congenial to the times. But in the first half of the nineteenth century the general common law also met a practical need. With an inactive federal legislature, there was no alternative to the courts if the rising commerce of the new nation was to have sure access to a uniform and hospitable body of law.

The success of the enterprise did not depend on the adoption of federally pronounced rules by state courts. As noted, foreign commerce was subject to the admiralty jurisdiction. Major domestic commercial transactions often enough were interstate. Disputes arising out of them were "Controversies . . . between Citizens of different

States." Under the diversity jurisdiction, such controversies could be adjudged in the federal courts under general common law.

The constitutional rationale of diversity jurisdiction was to protect the out-of-state suitor against local bias. Today we tend to think of the bias of the local tribunal—the judge or jury—but there is no reason in principle to exclude the bias of idiosyncratic local lawmakers. We may suppose that state legislatures and courts were in some degree responsive to local farmer and debtor interests as against the commercial classes of distant centers. It does not seem farfetched that federal judges, sitting in diversity, should find protection for absent creditors in the universal truths of the general common law—especially since politically the federal courts of the 1830s and 1840s were the last bastion of Federalist power. *Swift v. Tyson* itself strikes down a debtor's defense assertedly available under the law of New York, though there is perhaps less reason to suspect the New York legal system of populist fervor than that of some other states.

In any case, interest-based analysis is not crucial to my point. It seems clear to me that the federal judiciary exercised a substantial and needed general lawmaking power for the nation during these decades. It was a major source, perhaps the major source, of what might be called federal private law. Large-scale U.S. commercial activity, both national and international, grew and prospered as regulated by federal law, developed and administered by the federal courts.

Although *Swift v. Tyson* extended its sway far beyond its original domain of business and commercial matters, the country lived happily with it for almost half a century. The beginning of criticism toward the end of the nineteenth century coincides with the onset of the age of regulation, when both federal and state legislatures assumed an increasingly active lawmaking role. In such a positive law setting, with elected legislators making deliberately political choices about the regime of law applicable to corporations and persons, the notion of a neutral general common law, developed and applied by federal judges, became increasingly less viable, although it took another half century to administer the *coup de grâce.*

Erie R. Co. v. Tompkins, the case that did the deed, is presented to us as a sober and wise withdrawal of the federal courts from a realm of state power previously usurped. There is no doubt that the authority of federal courts to develop and declare the law applicable to interstate transactions was an important accretion of federal power vis-à-vis the states and would have been so understood by the framers. The Court of the 1930s that imposed these limits on the lawmaking powers of federal courts, however, was the same Court that struck down the constraints on federal legislative power elaborated by its predecessors. It is not clear that the states were net gainers from the exchange. In any event, *Erie* did not mark the end of the role of the federal courts in the governance of the nation.

Judicial Review. The power of the Supreme Court—and by extension lower federal courts—to declare acts of Congress void because in conflict with the Constitution was declared in 1803, before the country was two decades old. The Court first struck down a state law on this ground in 1809. Once announced, however, the power was sparingly used, and until the Civil War, only a handful of state or federal enactments had fallen.

Judicial review begins to assume its modern form only after the Civil War and the adoption of the postwar amendments. For the first time, the Constitution imposed substantial limitations directly upon the power of the states. The Court fumbled for a time in identifying the source of these constraints. The privileges and immunities clause seemed a possible candidate, but the Court denied itself in the *Slaughterhouse* cases. In *Munn* v. *Illinois*, it settled on the due process clause, although there it sustained the statute under attack. The stage setting was completed with *County of Santa Clara* v. *Southern Pac. R. Co.*, where, without hearing argument on the point, the Court held in a single paragraph that corporations are persons within the meaning of the clause and entitled to its protection, at least as to deprivations of property.

We are thus indebted to a conservative Court in a conservative age for the pregnant idea that the prohibition against deprivation of life, liberty, or property without due process of law is a limitation on the substantive power of state and federal legislatures and that this limitation is to be enforced by the courts.

For more than half a century, from the 1870s to the 1930s, the Supreme Court employed that idea against state and federal regulatory legislation designed to mitigate the rigors of the Industrial Revolution for workers and their families. The Court reached these results by a twofold doctrinal development. First, it developed the concept of property from its traditional moorings in tangible land or goods to cover a broad range of economic expectations. And second, it made the protection afforded those expectations increasingly absolute by raising the threshold of justification necessary to sustain legislation that impinged on them.

My generation of law students and most generations since were taught to regard this episode also as a usurpation, an interlude in an otherwise uniform history of judicial deference to legislative action. I have come to believe, however, that this characterization is erroneous.

In the first place, as I suggested above, in the first half-century of the republic the judiciary was an active federal lawmaking institution, perhaps more so than the Congress, certainly in the field of private law. Second, the earlier quiescence of the courts on the constitutional front derived more from the inactivity of legislatures and the absence of explicit constitutional limitations than from a posture of deference.

In my view, the turn-of-the-century Supreme Court was seeing and doing its duty as a constitutional court in a system in which the courts wield a share of the power to govern. Although there may have been error in the execution, there was no defect of principle. The words *liberty* and *property* in the Fourteenth Amendment are not self-defining; neither are the words *due process of law*. If, as has been almost uniformly supposed, the amendment is designed to place some limits on the power of elective institutions and if we are to accept John Marshall's exposition of the duty of the courts to say what the law is, then it falls to the federal courts, ultimately the Supreme Court, to give definition to those words, to say what the interests are that fall within the conceptions of liberty and property and what justification must be shown for their invasion.

There is no alternative except to say that the words mean nothing or are not judicially enforceable. But that conclusion is certainly at odds with *any* conception of our constitutional regime, including an originalist one. Whatever the framers may have thought about judicial review, by the time of the Civil War amendments, it was a going concern. That the drafters and ratifiers of the Fourteenth Amendment expected it to be a judicially enforceable limitation on the states is not open to doubt. Given that premise, however the catalog of liberties and the degree of enforcement are defined—broad or narrow, high or low—the definition is one that is ultimately judge made. The words of the amendment by themselves do not answer those questions.

In the period between the mid-1930s and the mid-1970s, the Supreme Court was performing the same task as its predecessors but answered the questions somewhat differently. It did not constrict the ambit of property. In fact, as in *Goldberg* v. *Kelley*, the conception retains considerable potential for continued growth. But the Court lowered the threshold of justification for legislative invasion of economic expectations. The process that is due in such cases is now hardly more than compliance with the formal requirements of legislative procedure. Given the realities of political representation and the susceptibility of economic interests to trade-off at the margin, the Court has concluded that the protections afforded these interests by the political process are by and large sufficient.

The striking phenomenon in the modern Court, however, is the

31

development of the notion of liberty from its base in physical mobility to comprise a wide range of autonomous personal activity. The process parallels that of the older Court with the concept of property.

The erection of the existing panoply of constitutionally protected liberties has taken place in my lifetime. The first time the First Amendment was seriously pressed as ground for the invalidation of a statute was in the draft cases in World War I. *Near* v. *Minnesota* in 1931 is the first case to strike down a statute as a violation of the right of free speech. The law in question imposed a classic prior restraint on publication. The Court first mandated the exclusion in a criminal trial of evidence obtained in violation of the Fourth Amendment in *Weeks* v. *United States* in 1914. The case marks the beginning of federal judicial oversight of federal and state criminal procedures.

Through the 1930s, the Court steadily extended the roll of personal freedoms implicit in a "regime of ordered liberty" and thus protected against state invasion. By the end of the 1940s the list included most of the guarantees of the Bill of Rights. Despite the strictures of Justice Black, however, the task of defining the meaning of liberty did not stop at that point, nor have we reached the end of the line today. Judicial definition of the array of protected liberties, like other processes of government, reaches no final stasis. Like other processes of government, it must and does respond over time to the changing situation and sentiments of the governed. Otherwise we would not now be celebrating the two hundredth anniversary of the structure contrived by the framers.

Affirmative Action. Constitutional adjudication is seen primarily as a negative function, the interposition of a judicial veto against legislative action. It may also be conceived as the affirmative process of bringing to fruition a system of liberty—of establishing justice. At the constitutional level, this affirmative conception has been given impetus by the emergence of the equal protection clause alongside the due process clause as a major basis of constitutional adjudication.

There is no textual ground for differentiating between the two in this respect. The command of the Fourteenth Amendment is the same as to both. It is a negative injunction, forbidding the state to "deprive" any person of due process or to "deny" to any person equal protection. But equal protection of the laws is not a free good out there, available to anyone unless invaded or curtailed by the state. The protection of the laws is something provided in the first instance by the state, and the obligation not to deny it is implicitly an affirmative obligation to provide it on equal terms.

The obligation is not discharged by a merely formal equality.

Anatole France, speaking of "the majestic equality of the law, which prevents the rich and poor alike from sleeping under the bridges of Paris,"[1] was not celebrating the equal protection of the laws. There is thus an inherent affirmative spin in equal protection jurisprudence. The task of establishing justice is not simply to prevent the state from doing something wrong but to try to make sure it does it right.

Problems arise not because judges are engaged in the effort but because of the difficulty of the enterprise. Legislatures as well as courts find it hard to induce affirmative action for defined social ends. It is much easier for government to prohibit undesired activity, to enforce negative commands, than to elicit desired responses. Nevertheless, for fifty years, some would say twice that, the United States has been committed to the use of government as an instrument to achieve politically defined social and economic objectives.

Despite some retrenchment in recent years, which in truth has been more rhetorical than real, that commitment has not been withdrawn. In this respect we are no different from other Western democracies. In fact, a meliorative reformist propensity may well be inherent in any government based on popular democracy. (The conclusion would not have surprise the framers, though it would not have been welcomed equally by all of them.)

So it is in the implementation of statutory regulation rather than on the constitutional plane that the judicial department first and most broadly enters the arena of affirmative action. There, it does so as partner rather than antagonist of the Congress. When the legislature no longer confines itself to preventing bad acts but seeks to induce good ones, it faces a formidable drafting problem. The relative clarity and precision of Austinian "thou shalt nots" is no longer available. Congress is reduced to defining the policy objectives of legislation, sketching in the main lines of implementation, and resolving some of the specific issues that have risen above the political noise during the legislative process. The rest it remits perforce to courts or administrative agencies, subject in our system to the supervision of the courts.

The Sherman Act, the first or almost the first federal regulatory statute, is a paradigmatic case. Congress, seeking to promote a competitive economy, prohibited every contract, combination, or conspiracy in restraint of trade, leaving the enforcement of the statute to proceedings in the federal courts. Almost all the substantive content of that regulation has been worked out by the courts.

On some matters, mostly in the constitutional area, the Court has announced a policy of "clear statement." There are occasional suggestions that courts should "remand" excessively murky statutes to the legislature, although nobody has said exactly how that would be done.

It has not proved possible, however, to change legislative practice. In the antitrust area, for example, Congress returns to the task from time to time. It has sought to clarify particular issues that have emerged, and it has given pieces of the job to other agencies, notably the Federal Trade Commission. But antitrust law remains predominantly an artifact of the federal judiciary. More broadly, I would propose that in the interpretation and application of regulatory statutes, the federal judiciary has created a body of judge-made law at least as extensive, *mutatis mutandis,* as the general common law of the *Swift* v. *Tyson* era.

Some of this corpus reflects judicial determination of the *meaning* of language enacted by Congress, a technical, but by no means mechanical task. In large part, though, elaborating substantive statutory provisions is not so different from what common law courts have traditionally done in working out the implications of general legal principles or even in interpreting ordinary contracts. Concepts or words of broad and indeterminate import are given specific meaning in the context of a particular case.

By tradition, however, our courts sit not only to say what the law is but also to grant relief for its violation. Where, as in the case of most regulatory legislation, the law has an affirmative policy, a desired end state, relief cannot stop with a simple negative command, any more than the original enactment can. To enforce the law is to try to vindicate the policy embodied in it. That may require affirmative action, not merely forbearance, from the defendant. So in the antitrust cases, the Court not only enjoined future conduct that it had found violative of the statute but also ordered defendants to divest wrongfully acquired assets, to license freely patents that had been used for illegal purposes, to introduce new terms and conditions into dealers' and distributors' contracts, and to take other affirmative action to establish competitive markets. When a violation of the basic regulatory scheme was established, it brought to life a considerable arsenal of remedial and corrective authority, not otherwise available to courts.

A similar account could be given of the role of courts in many other areas of regulation—antidiscrimination laws, environmental controls, health and safety legislation, and the like. Only slight adjustments are needed to make the story fit regulatory programs where action in the first instance is consigned to administrative agencies.

The case is no different when the federal courts are asked to review conduct of officials administering public institutions. The most profound and far-reaching intervention of this kind has been the work of desegregating the nation's public schools and other public facilities. Thirty-five years after *Brown* v. *Board of Education*, it is hard to imagine how legally enforced segregation on the basis of race could ever have been squared with the most elementary idea of equal protection of the laws. Once the Court was prepared to pronounce this principle and local school boards had failed or refused to respond, it was no conceptual stretch to call upon the reservoir of remedial power that had already been developed in the regulatory field.

With prisons, jails, mental hospitals, homes for the mentally retarded, and other such public institutions in this area, there was no need to create new constitutional rights. It was surely no great leap to say that to confine a person in subhuman conditions, whatever the reason for the confinement, is a deprivation of liberty without due process of law. Nor have the courts in such cases set themselves against the legislative will. Statutes establishing such institutions commonly provide that they shall be conducted in a humane manner and that the inmates shall be cared for so as to promote rehabilitation or cure. In the 1970s the federal courts began to mobilize their remedial resources to achieve those legislatively stipulated objectives.

In neither desegregation nor institutional confinement has judicial intervention successfully transformed the defendant institutions and bureaucracies. That is agreed by both the critics and those who activated the courts in the first place.

Why should that surprise anyone? It is the fate of all reformist enterprises that they cannot fundamentally change the institutions with which they deal, a proposition Edmund Burke would endorse. They can, however, induce changes at the margin, improve, and set new directions and new criteria for judgment.

In the civil rights and institutional cases, the most important result of judicial action has been to energize the Congress and state legislatures, to change legislative agendas, to force reconsideration of spending and resource allocation, to transform the terms of public debate, and to lubricate the processes of change. The judicial department does not govern by itself; it shares in the work.

An Active Judiciary

You will notice that I have described an active judiciary. I maintain that this institutional outcome is implicit in the decision of the framers to create the federal judicial branch as a department of government, on an equal plane with the legislative and executive, and thus to vest it with a share of the power to govern. The judicial branch has exercised this power in different ways in response to different requirements of the society at different times in its history:

- At first it created a system of federal private law.
- From the property rights and liberty of contract of nineteenth-century entrepreneurs to the right of privacy in the anonymity of a crowded contemporary urban environment, it has defined an expanding array of personal liberties and defended them against government encroachment.
- It joins with Congress and the administrative agencies in the administration of the regulatory state.
- It deploys affirmative remedial techniques in the service of positive social objectives validated by Constitution and statute.

In whatever form, the federal judiciary, throughout American history, has been an active participant in governing the country. I believe that is what the founders intended. The institutional response of the judiciary, however, has been driven more by the practical and pragmatic needs of government than by theory.

The framers said they wanted to create a government of laws and not of men, and they succeeded. We have had a good deal of soul searching in recent years about the resulting "juristocracy" of ours. By no means have all the conclusions been favorable. Although this is a celebratory occasion, I have no quarrel with much of the criticism. Judges are not immune from error, as all of them who do not sit on the Supreme Court soon find out. Even about the Supreme Court, Justice Jackson said, "We are not final because we are infallible; we are infallible because we are final."[2] And the federal judiciary as an institution is, like all human institutions, radically imperfect.

There are things to be said for a "law-ridden" society, though. For one thing, when law is the social integument, there is a feedback effect. Law and justice become the concern of legislators and officials and common people, not just the courts. That does not render America proof against official lawlessness, as we have had recent occasion to observe. But I take a certain pride when European friends, with different legal or judicial systems, profess not to understand how we can make such a public fuss about it.

For another thing, law is not static. It changes and grows in a symbiotic relationship with the society. This process of change and growth merits attention. Attorney General Meese took a good deal of criticism for his recent statement that the Constitution was not necessarily what the Supreme Court says it is. I do not see how anyone could disagree with that, certainly not any law professor. Our most sacred professional prerogative is to be able to tell students the Supreme Court is wrong.

Much of the history of expanding liberty we justly celebrate was made by people who refused to accept the Constitution as the Supreme Court said it was. Jehovah's Witnesses challenged the compulsory schoolroom flag salute five times in the Supreme Court before it was declared unconstitutional. Three times the case was dismissed "for want of a substantial federal question."[3] Then the Court after plenary consideration upheld the practice with only Justice Jackson dissenting. Finally, *West Virginia Board of Education* v. *Barnette* held such a requirement to be inconsistent with First Amendment freedom of religion.

Challenge to established doctrine is an engine of growth in the law, and we should not choke it off. The Jehovah's Witnesses, though, were in a different position from the U.S. government. They had to violate the law—to exercise the "right" of civil disobedience—in order to create the case or controversy that would get them into court. The executive, in my view, does not need and has no right of civil disobedience. While the government is free to challenge an existing reading of the Constitution or any other law—and it has often done so with great benefit to all—it is not free to violate the law in order to do so. Nor is it free to decide for itself what law shall govern its actions, without regard to the law on the books. It is bound until the law is changed.

Finally, we may ask, what is the active principle that governs change in the law? And what is the safeguard against error?

It is not the vote. The Supreme Court, as Mr. Dooley said, reads the election returns, but it is not bound by them. That would not, I think, have unduly disturbed the framers. They were by no means wholly enamored of the vote as a universal solvent. Neither the president nor the Senate, in the original plan, was chosen by direct suffrage. So although we take a just pride in our democracy, we need not always find ultimate wisdom in the decisions of a transitory political majority.

An approach to the problem of the ultimate check on judicial power is to return to our original question: How does the Constitution establish justice? We all know the answer to that question: it does not. As a society, we have been working at establishing justice on and off for 200 years, and we still have not accomplished it. We can take some pride in that effort—but not too much. Although America is a more just society than most today or that we know historically, our society still contains much that is an affront to justice, too much to warrant any self-satisfaction.

That is another way of saying that justice, like any other animating human ideal, can never be achieved. Indeed, it can never even be comprehensively defined.

What the framers established was a process for seeking after justice. It is a process in which law and judges, rightly I think, play the central role. Alexander Bickel reminded us of Hamilton's statement that the judiciary is "the least dangerous branch"[4]—and I would add the most powerful: least dangerous, because the judgment of a court, like poetry, "makes nothing happen."[5]

But why the most powerful? Richard Neustadt said, "The power of the President is the power to persuade."[6] And if that is true of the power of the president, how much so of the power of the courts? Nothing the Supreme Court does or says really makes anything happen unless it ultimately persuades us that it is right. That was Bickel's basic point.

Unlike the president, the Court does not seek to persuade bureaucrats or legislators or even voters about immediate responses to this or that program or crisis. It speaks to all of us, and it speaks about the basic values that define us as a nation and a society. It seeks to persuade us at the deepest and most fundamental level. That is why, in the long run, it is the most powerful branch.

Let me conclude with a story. Learned Hand was visiting Washington and went out to lunch with Justice Holmes. They walked back to the Capitol, where the Court still sat. As they parted, Hand called after Holmes, "Do justice."

The old man turned on him fiercely, eyebrows bristling: "What's that? What's that? That's none of my business. *Law* is my business." What else would we expect of the Holmes who promulgated the "bad man theory of the law"[7] many years earlier in *The Path of the Law?* The point is the same: law and justice inhabit different worlds.

But we know that is not true: we know that law is inevitably concerned with justice. There is no way to talk about law without coming in the end to talk about justice.

It is not that we agree on what justice is—although it is interesting how often our ideas and instincts converge. The idea of justice, however, provides a point of view outside the system from which we can criticize it, an Archimedean platform for exerting leverage to change it.

Of course, the joke of the story is on Holmes. We revere him and celebrate him not because he was a superb technical lawyer and judge—although he certainly was. He is a folk hero—America is the only country in the world that has judges for folk heroes, and they all share this characteristic. Holmes is a folk hero because he was a fighter for justice or we see him so. What resonates for us are the great cadences of the *Lochner* and *Abrams* dissents and others in which he used his craft in the law to explore the meaning of justice. His utterances—and those of the other hero-judges—help keep the discourse of justice alive for us.

That is how the Constitution establishes justice.

Notes

1. Anatole France, *The Red Lily* (The Modern Library ed., 1917), p. 75.

2. See Brown v. Allen, 344 U.S. 443, 540 (1953) (Jackson, J., concurring in result).

3. See Johnson v. Deerfield, 306 U.S. 621 (1939); Hering v. State Board of Education, 303 U.S. 624 (1938); Leoles v. Landers, 302 U.S. 656 (1937).

4. Alexander Bickel, *The Least Dangerous Branch* (New Haven, Conn.: Yale University Press, 1962), p. 1. Bickel adapted the phrase from Hamilton's famous passage in *Federalist* No. 78: "Whoever attentively considers the different departments of power must perceive, that . . . the judiciary, from the nature of its functions, will always be the least dangerous." See *The Federalist* No. 78 (J. Cooke ed., 1961), p. 522.

5. W. H. Auden, "In Memory of W. B. Yeats," in *W. H. Auden: Collected Poems,* ed. Edward Mendelson (New York: Random House, 1976), p. 197. Bickel refers to the same verse. See Bickel, *The Least Dangerous Branch,* p. 245.

6. Richard Neustadt, *Presidential Power: The Politics of Leadership from FDR to Carter* (New York: Macmillan, 1960), p. 10.

7. See Oliver Wendell Holmes, "The Path of the Law," *Harvard Law Review,* vol. 10 (1897), pp. 457, 459.

3
Justice as the Securing of Rights
Walter Berns

If this were the place to go into details, I would easily explain how, even without the involvement of government, inequality of credit and authority becomes inevitable between individuals as soon as, united in the same society, they are forced to make comparisons between themselves and to take into account differences they find in the continual use they have to make of one another. These differences are of several kinds; but in general wealth, nobility or rank, power, and personal merit being the principal distinctions by which one is measured in society, I would prove that the agreement or conflict of these various forces is the surest indication of a well- or ill-constituted state. I would show that of these four types of inequality, as personal qualities are the origin of all the others, wealth is the last to which they are reduced in the end because, being the most immediately useful to well-being and the easiest to communicate, it is easily used to buy all the rest. . . .

JEAN-JACQUES ROUSSEAU

The Constitution of the United States was adopted, in part, to "establish Justice," but it was not until 1870 that Congress got around to establishing a Department of Justice—and even then it gave no clue as to what it meant by justice. The enabling statute consisted mainly of provisions transferring already existing legal offices to the newly established department and establishing new offices—for example, the office of solicitor general—to assist the attorney general in the performance of his duties.[1]

Those duties had remained essentially unchanged since 1789 when, by the first Judiciary Act, the various justice offices were established: the U.S. attorneys (one in each judicial district) were to prosecute "all delinquents for crimes and offences, cognizable under the authority of the United States, and all civil actions in which the United States shall be concerned"; and the attorney general—"a meet person, learned in the law"—in addition to serving as legal adviser to the president and the heads of departments, was to "prosecute and conduct all suits in the Supreme Court in which the United States shall be concerned."[2] In short, the attorney general and his assistants, originally and in the newly created department, were to be concerned with only a part of justice, the part to which Aristotle gave the name "corrective justice." They were to have no jurisdiction over matters having to do with "distributive justice."[3] In fact, although the point will have to be amplified, the Constitution itself seems to have little or nothing to do with distributive justice.

Corrective (or commutative) justice, for Aristotle as well as for his modern successors, has to do with private transactions, such as buying and selling, and treats men as equals:

> For it makes no difference whether a good man has defrauded a bad man or a bad one a good one, nor whether it is a good or a bad man that has committed adultery; the law looks only at the nature of the damage, treating the parties as equals, and merely asking whether one has done and the other suffered injustice, whether one inflicted and the other sustained damage.[4]

Thomas Hobbes, the first of the philosophers of natural rights, had no quarrel with this analysis, at least not formally: "To speak properly, commutative justice, is the justice, of a contractor; that is, a performance of covenant, in buying, and selling; hiring, and letting to hire; lending, and borrowing; exchanging, bartering, and other acts of contract."[5]

Distributive justice, in contrast, has to do with the "distribution of honour, wealth, and the other divisible assets of the community," as Aristotle puts it, including, of course, political offices or power, and these assets "may be allotted among its members in equal or unequal shares."[6] A proper or fair allotment, however, will recognize that men are more or less worthy—of office, honor, or whatever—or more or less virtuous. In other words, distributive justice in the classical sense recognizes the inequality of men and is prepared to treat them unequally. It depends on at least one judgment that Hobbes was among the first to insist could not fairly or rightly be made: the judgment that some men are intrinsically more deserving than others. From this Hobbes concluded that the distinction between distributive and commutative justice "is not right."[7]

Justice, according to Hobbes, is only commutative justice, giving men that which *belongs* to them or rewarding or punishing them in accordance with their actions, equally, without regard to their worth or presumed worth. Distributive justice in Aristotle's sense simply disappears; it becomes the justice of an arbitrator who distributes to every man his own and, as Hobbes says, is more properly called "equity." Or, stated otherwise, distributive justice for Hobbes is the distribution of rewards and punishments according to the rules of commutative justice.[8]

In saying this, Hobbes is merely drawing a conclusion consistent with his premise, which is that civil society originates in a covenant entered into by men who are by nature equal, insofar as they are equally endowed with rights. It is this that makes his analysis relevant to the American experience. A government based on the self-evident truth that all men are created equal insofar as they are equally endowed "with certain unalienable rights" and instituted "to secure these rights" is obliged to treat everybody equally with respect to those rights. It would appear that the Constitution sees justice as the securing of rights. Whether that is a viable understanding remains to be seen.

Rights under the Constitution

The framers were under no illusions that establishing this justice would be a simple matter. To secure rights means, first of all, recognizing and respecting the private realm those rights define or describe, a realm into which the public with its laws and controls may not enter. Congress shall make *no* law, reads the First Amendment, "respecting an establishment of religion, or prohibiting the free exercise thereof; or abridging the freedom of speech, or of the press." What a person does with the rights secured by the Constitution—for example, how or what he worships, what he says, or what he does with the money he earns or inherits—is none of the public's business. What is done in that private realm may be done *without* the consent of the governed—unless, of course, what is done is "adverse to the rights of other citizens, or to the permanent and aggregate interests of the community," to quote *Federalist* 10. In saying this, Madison reminds us that, like it or not, security for private rights requires a community, and justice requires that its interests be given due consideration.

Prominent among these permanent interests is the community's capacity to defend itself against its enemies. "Among the many objects to which a wise and free people find it necessary to direct their attention," wrote John Jay in *Federalist* 3, "that of providing for their *safety* seems to be the first," and he expected the most immediate threat to the nation's security to come from foreign arms and influence. To meet it, the nation must be prepared to arm itself. Unfortunately, however, people inspired by the idea of private rights are more likely to claim their rights and, indeed, to claim an expanded notion of their rights, than they are to make the sacrifices required to provide for the public safety. According to Alexander Hamilton, "The industrious habits of the people of the present day, absorbed in the pursuits of gain and devoted to the improvements of agriculture and commerce, are incompatible with the condition of a nation of soldiers."[9] It would come as no surprise to him to learn that, in time, the people (or at least some of them) would resist conscription into the armed forces, claiming it to be a form of involuntary servitude; or would claim a right to be exempted from military service not only on religious grounds but also on the basis of pacifist views acquired by a reading "of history and sociology"; or would claim that college students have a right to federal financial aid even if they refuse to register for the draft; or, speaking as the American Civil Liberties Union, would claim that "a citizen has the right to impair or impede the functions of a Government agency, whether it is the Federal Trade Commission or the CIA."[10]

Establishing this justice is made even more difficult by the fact that the community is composed of men who are *un*equal in so many respects. They may be equal in their possession of rights, and be as one in the desire to secure them, but they are likely to be sharply divided in other respects; equality of rights does not imply equality of faculties or equality of interest, sentiment, or passion. With respect to these qualities or characteristics, their differences are marked and can be critical. According to John Locke—"America's philosopher," as he is sometimes called—men living in the state of nature can be put in one of two categories, "the industrious and rational" or "the quarrelsome and contentious," and, because the latter are more numerous, the state of nature comes to resemble the state of war. "To avoid this state of war," Locke writes, "is one great reason of men's putting themselves into society and quitting the state of nature."[11] The framers knew, however, that unless great care is taken when founding that society, the "quarrelsome and contentious" in nature will become an "interested and overbearing majority" under government. As James Madison writes in the celebrated *Federalist* 10,

> Complaints are everywhere heard from our most considerate and virtuous citizens, equally the friends of public and private faith and of public and personal liberty, that our governments are too unstable, that the public good is disregarded in the conflicts of rival parties, and that measures are too often decided, not according to the rules of justice

and the rights of the minor party, but by the superior force of an interested and overbearing majority."[12]

On the next page Madison indicates why such differences are not readily resolved and why justice is not readily obtained. He had learned from Locke that men are naturally and primarily inclined to seek the "conveniences and comforts of Life"; this inclination, Locke said, derives from "the strongest desire God Planted in Men, and wrought into the very Principles of their Nature," that of "Self-Preservation."[13] It followed for Locke and for Madison as well that a government instituted to secure rights is obliged to protect the right to acquire property, or the "conveniences and comforts of Life." When the right is protected—which will have the effect of encouraging men to do what they are naturally inclined to do—they will employ their faculties in the task of acquiring the good things of this world, as someone once said. Madison does not hesitate to say that the "first object of government" is the protection of these faculties when they are so employed, even though men are unequally endowed with them. "From the protection of different and unequal faculties of acquiring property," he writes, "the possession of different degrees and kinds of property immediately results; and from the influence of these on the sentiments and views of the respective proprietors ensues a division of the society into different interests and parties."[14]

In other words, because men are by nature unequally endowed with the faculties by which property is acquired—strength, energy, intelligence, pertinacity, determination, boldness, or whatever—the just society will be one in which property and wealth are unequally distributed. To that extent, it conforms to Aristotle's description of distributive justice. Here in America, however, the distribution is made directly by nature, not by the government following nature (or claiming to follow nature). By securing the equal rights of unequally endowed men, the government simply allows nature to take its course. Beyond this, it must somehow persuade the people, and especially the less well-endowed among them, that nature is fair; it must persuade them that an unequal distribution of property is compatible with justice. If Rousseau is correct, however, when he says (in the epigraph) that with wealth the other goods—rank, power, and personal merit—can be purchased, persuading them of this might prove to be very difficult indeed.[15]

Controlling Democratic Envy

In the event, it has proved easy in America—compared with the task confronting the governments of the other democracies, very easy.

Alexis de Tocqueville saw this 150 years ago. "Why is it," he asked, "that in America, the land par excellence of democracy, no one makes that outcry against property in general that often echoes throughout Europe?" His answer would have confounded Karl Marx. "It is because there are no proletarians in America"[16]—no proletarians, no class struggle, no widespread dissatisfaction with the quality of American justice or the fairness of nature's dispensation. Democratic envy would exist, but it would not be politically dangerous; the framers could not remove its causes, but they could find a way of controlling its effects.

How, precisely, this was accomplished, or would be accomplished, is explained in great detail in *The Federalist*, especially in *Federalist* 10. Powers are separated; the legislative power is divided between two branches, one of them representing the states without regard to the size of their populations; and the people are represented in a way that distinguishes the American from the constitutions of all previous republics. No federal official or collection of officials is elected by the people at large, or by the whole body of the people; because votes are not aggregated at the national level, no federal official—neither the president nor any number of senators or members of the House of Representatives—can claim to represent, or can be said to represent, *"the people in their collective capacity,"* as Madison put it in *Federalist* 63. Collectively, the people are totally excluded, he said. In a word, the constitutional structure inhibits the formation of popular majorities of the people, but it does this without relying on aristocratic or nonpopular institutions or, following Aristotle's principle of distributive justice, on an unequal distribution of honors and offices.

Such a principle was espoused by some delegates to the Constitutional Convention. Pierce Butler and John Rutledge of South Carolina, Abraham Baldwin of Georgia, Gouverneur Morris of Pennsylvania, and George Mason of Virginia were among the delegates who argued, unsuccessfully, that "wealth as well as numbers of Free Inhabitants" ought to be represented. "One important object in constituting the Senate," Mason observed, "was to secure the rights of property."[17] John Dickinson of Pennsylvania said he wished the Senate "to consist of the most distinguished characters, distinguished for their rank in life and their weight of property, and bearing as strong a likeness to the British House of Lords as possible"—and the more of such persons, the better. He adhered, he said, "to the opinion that the Senate ought to be composed of a large number, and that their influence from family weight & other causes would be increased thereby." His colleague from Pennsylvania, James Wilson, responded, however, with the simple and telling observation that America lacked the "materials" for an aristocratic assembly. There were, and there would be, no great American families: "Our manners, our laws, the abolition of entails and of primogeniture, the whole genius of the people, are opposed to it."[18] Such families, if they ever existed in any numbers, left with the Tories.

Wilson and Madison were not unsympathetic with the idea of a Senate with "weight"—such a body was needed to balance the weight of democratic numbers in the House of Representatives—but weight could not be had simply by multiplying the number of senators. In the absence of a hereditary nobility or a property franchise, the larger the number of senators, the more they would resemble their democratic constituents, and the more the Senate would resemble the House of Representatives. So said Madison, and it was he who drew the conclusion: "When the weight of a set of men depends merely on their personal characters; the greater the number the greater the weight. When it depends on the degree of political authority lodged in them the smaller the number the greater the weight."[19] So it was that the Senate was kept small and the senators given longer terms and, in their authority to advise and consent to treaties and appointments, significantly greater power than that given the members of the House.

These various institutions—separation of powers, checks and balances, representation, together with an independent judiciary—were intended to give the union a "proper structure"; and structure combined with the very size of the country would make it difficult for democratic envy or resentment to become a national political force. The rebellions of the future, like the one led by Daniel Shays, would be local in their scope and effects. As Madison said in *Federalist* 10, "A rage for paper money, for the abolition of debts, for an equal division of property, or for any other improper or wicked project, will be less apt to pervade the whole body of the Union than a particular member of it, in the same proportion as such a malady is more likely to taint a particular county or district than an entire State." In size and proper structure they saw a remedy for "the diseases most incident to republican government," and, as Madison took great pride in pointing out, it was "a republican remedy": no monarch, no House of Lords, no constitutional restrictions on the suffrage.

Underlying this structure, however, was a program designed specifically to address the complaint of unfairness in the distribution of material goods or wealth. Fashioned by Adam Smith from principles discovered by John Locke, this was a program intended to promote economic growth and thereby put an end to the economic scarcity that had previously governed political life. Aristotle took it for granted that there would be a scarcity of material goods; that assumption underlies his analysis of distributive justice. When he speaks of the "common property," or the "common stock," or "honour, wealth, and the other divisible assets of the community, which may be allotted among its members in equal or unequal shares," he assumes a fixed amount, or a limited supply, of the goods to be distributed. Under such circumstances, giving to one means taking from or depriving another; it means in practice that the rich will have an interest in keeping the poor down and that the poor will have an interest in bringing down the rich. This is not true in America: not with economic growth; not with an ever-growing gross national product; not where everyone has the right to acquire property and the reasonable expectation that he will succeed; not where everyone is encouraged to be *busy.* "The prosperity of commerce," writes Alexander Hamilton in *Federalist* 12, "is now perceived and acknowledged by all enlightened statesmen to be the most useful as well as the most productive source of national wealth, and has accordingly become a primary object of their political cares." He explains the reason for this in the sequel:

> By multiplying the means of gratification, by promoting the introduction and circulation of the precious metals, those darling objects of human avarice and enterprise, it serves to vivify and invigorate all the channels of industry and to make them flow with greater activity and copiousness. The assiduous merchant, the laborious husbandman, the active mechanic, and the industrious manufacturer—all orders of men look forward with eager expectation and growing alacrity to this pleasing reward of their toils.

This new program was, of course, intended to provide a relief of man's estate, to improve his material conditions; and that it has certainly done. But it was also, perhaps even primarily, designed with a view to the expected political consequences. Economic growth would allay resentment and thereby make it easier to secure rights and establish justice. That it had these consequences in America Tocqueville was one of the first to see:

> The American man of the people has conceived a high idea of political rights because he has some; he does not attack those of others, in order that his own may not be violated. Whereas the corresponding man in Europe would be prejudiced against all authority, even the highest, the American uncomplainingly obeys the lowest of his officials.[20]

Justice and Black Americans and Indians

In promoting their project, the framers made one assumption: they assumed that Americans, being a civilized people, possessed the qualities needed for its success. About the moral habits or the civic virtues that make it possible to live together in a free and democratic community the framers made no assumptions; they acknowledged the necessity and, to some extent at least, sought means to meet it. What they did assume was that the typical American was capable of exercising his rights or of using the freedom afforded him when his rights were secured. A statement of Abraham Lincoln's serves to illustrate the point: the Civil War, he said, "is a struggle for maintaining in the world, that form, and substance of government, whose leading object is, to elevate the condition of men." As he goes right on to say, however, that is to be done by "lift[ing] artificial weights from all shoulders—to clear the paths of laudable pursuit for all—to afford all, an unfettered start, and a fair chance, in the race of life."[21] Presumably, men are held back only by "artificial" weights or fetters, and once these are removed—and they are removed when rights are secured—they can all run a good race.

This sense of the matter is implicit in the way our rights are stated in the Declaration of Independence and more evidently in the Constitution: to acquire a knowledge of the truth or the keys to heaven, wealth or the means to a happy private life, all we ask of government is that it make no law "respecting an establishment of religion, or prohibiting the free exercise thereof; or abridging the freedom of speech, or of the press"; or that it not deprive us of "property, without due process of law"; or that it not subject "our persons, houses, papers, and effects [to] unreasonable searches and seizures." As Nathan Tarcov made clear in a chapter written for an earlier volume in this series, we have rights to do, keep, or acquire things, as well as rights *not* to have things *done* to us or *taken from* us, but not rights to have things *done* or *given* to us.[22] Unlike the Soviet, our Constitution does not speak of "the right to work, that is, the right to guaranteed employment and payment . . . in accordance with its quantity and quality."[23] This is why, unlike the Soviet, our government is not obliged to find jobs for us (if necessary in Siberia). We ask of government only that it provide the security and with it the liberty that make it possible for us to go about our business, so to speak. And especially in our early years, we went about it energetically.

Many a European visitor took note of this quality. Landing in New York in May 1831, Gustave de Beaumont, for one, was struck by the "busyness" of the place. "It's quite a remarkable phenomenon," he wrote his father, "a great people which has no army, a country full of activity and vigour where the action of the government is hardly perceived."[24] There is no established church but, as Madison foresaw, a "multiplicity of sects" and a sufficiency of righteousness; no government monopolies, but a "multiplicity of interests" and a cornucopia of material goods.[25] Tocqueville, Beaumont's more famous companion, said much the same thing in a letter to *his* father:

> Everybody works, and the mine is still so rich that all those who work rapidly succeed in acquiring that which renders existence happy. The most active spirits, like the most tranquil, find enough to fill their life here without busying themselves troubling the state. The restlessness which so wracks our European societies seems to co-operate toward the prosperity of this one. It aims only at wealth, and finds a thousand roads which lead there.[26]

An inactive government and an active, prosperous, and apparently happy people—by securing the rights of a civilized people justice is done, and wonders can be achieved. And the framers assumed that the typical American was civilized.

They drew an altogether different conclusion about the native Americans and the blacks. To Thomas Jefferson, who had studied them and their languages with great care, the Indians were uncivilized and unfit, or not yet fit, to be part of the people of the United States. In his book *Notes on the State of Virginia*, he treated the subject of the Indians in a chapter devoted to the region's natural resources: minerals, plants, fruits, wild animals, and the "aborigines." He said that in mind and body they were as well formed as Europeans but that they had no experience of law or government; for them, as for every other "barbarous people," force was law, which explained why their women, the weaker sex, were subjected to "unjust drudgery." Taking his cue from Locke, Jefferson seemed to be suggesting that only as men develop those faculties that distinguish them from the inferior animals—in short, only as they become civilized—can they devise the means of securing their rights and can they utilize the possibilities afforded by that security.[27]

He drew much the same conclusion about the blacks, except that here he entertained the suspicion that not even time would rid them of their disabilities. "I advance it," he said, "as a suspicion only, that the blacks, whether originally a distinct race, or made distinct by time and circumstances, are inferior to the whites in the endowments both of mind and body."[28] He could not deny their humanity, however; blacks were men and were endowed with the rights of men, and it was "execrable" that white Americans should be allowed "to trample" on these rights. By doing so, they transformed themselves into "despots" and the blacks into "enemies."[29] Blacks may have lacked (or not yet acquired) the talents of civilized men, but "Whatever be their degree of talent it is no measure of their rights." Jefferson said it was

49

inevitable, "written in the book of fate," that they would one day be free, but, sadly, no "less certain that the two races [black and white], equally free, cannot live in the same government."[30] In saying this, Jefferson probably spoke for the founders in general.[31]

He was, of course, mistaken. Freedom for black Americans came with the Thirteenth Amendment and citizenship—along with certain privileges, immunities, and rights—came with the Fourteenth, but except in these formal respects their situation was not much changed after the Civil War. The states were now forbidden to deprive black as well as white persons of property without due process of law, for example, but it did not occur to many people in authority—Abraham Lincoln was an exception—to wonder whether black persons as yet possessed the capacity, education, knowledge, and talents required to acquire property in the first place. Could justice be done simply by treating them equally, which is to say, simply by securing their right to be left alone? The question was not seriously considered. In the event, little or nothing was done to save the freedmen from the "vagrant destitution" that Lincoln feared would be their lot, and proved to be their lot for generations.

Redistributing Assets

By lifting the "artificial weights" of slavery from their shoulders, had the country in fact afforded black citizens "an unfettered start and a fair chance in the race of life"? That question could not forever be suppressed, especially after the blacks began to vote in great numbers. The answer was, of course, obvious. As a class—a category that does not, however, exist in the eyes of the Constitution—they deserved something more than the right to be left alone to go about their business. The assistance that ought to have been offered after the Civil War, however, as an act of charity or love, is now being claimed—and extended—as a right, a right to a certain share of "the honors, wealth, and the other divisible assets of the community." In the eyes of the Constitution, this is a new kind of right.

The right to vote is no longer simply the right to cast a ballot, free from discrimination or intimidation, and to have it counted; it is now, in addition, the right to cast a nondiluted ballot, meaning, among other things, "a right to a form of proportional representation in favor of all geographically and politically cohesive minority groups that are large enough to constitute majorities if concentrated within one or more single-member districts."[32] This says, in effect, that one's right to vote includes the right to be represented by members of one's class or race.

Welfare benefits are no longer a kind of public charity dispensed by a compassionate legislature; they are "property rights" and may not be terminated without a due process hearing.[33] Courts have even allowed suits by recipients to increase benefits, thereby recognizing a "right" to those benefits; but as R. Shep Melnick has pointed out, they have not yet allowed suits by taxpayers to reduce them.[34]

A statute forbidding discrimination "against any individual with respect to his compensation, terms, conditions, or privileges of employment, because of such individual's race, color, religion, sex, or national origin" is converted by the Supreme Court, with the implicit consent of a compliant Congress, into a statute that permits and in most cases requires such discrimination. That is to say, a right to seek a job, regardless of one's race or sex, becomes a right to a job because of one's race or sex. As Justice Antonin Scalia said in dissent in the case that completed this process of conversion, the employment plan (upheld by the majority of the Court) "did not seek to replicate what a lack of discrimination would produce, but rather imposed racial and sexual tailoring that would, in defiance of normal expectations and laws of probability, give each protected racial and sexual group a governmentally determined 'proper' proportion of each job category."[35]

Quite clearly, the American government has embarked on a program of distributing (or redistributing) at least some of the "divisible assets of the community." The program was initiated specifically to repair the damage caused by the injustices and other mistakes of the past, but redistribution would have come eventually even if slavery had never existed in this country and even if, after the Civil War, our policy had not been largely one of neglect. At some point, sooner or later, there would have been a political demand for a fairer (or more equal) distribution of material goods. The Constitution may not recognize a principle of distributive justice, and the securing of rights, as we have traditionally understood the nature of those rights, may be incompatible with this new dispensation, but the demand for it would eventually have been irrepressible.

Tocqueville knew that. As he said, "The progress of equality is something fated." It is, he went on, something passing beyond human control: "Does anyone imagine that democracy, which has destroyed the feudal system and vanquished kings, will fall back before the middle classes and the rich? Will it stop now, when it has grown so strong and its adversaries so weak?"[36] In a word, political equality would bring in its wake an economic equality; no constitutional structure would forever be able to prevail against it. The wonder is that, in this country, it was so long in coming.

51

A few years ago, Harvard philosophy professor John Rawls proclaimed that justice is fairness, and the slogan was quickly picked up by the academic community.[37] His most celebrated devotee among academic lawyers, Ronald Dworkin, followed with the assertion that, thanks to Rawls, it was possible for the first time to infuse constitutional law with moral theory. Accordingly, the Constitution would now be able to recognize not only the rights of conscientious objection and civil disobedience (without penalty) but the fundamental right to "equal concern and respect."[38] To secure *this* right would require government intervention on a scale not yet experienced or, by most of us, even imagined: not only wealth, but honors ("concern and respect") would have to be redistributed, and this would involve the government in a fight against nature. It would probably require the sort of government Tocqueville warned against at the end of *Democracy in America*. He called it a soft despotism:

> Over this kind of men stands an immense, protective power which is alone responsible for securing their enjoyment and watching over their fate. That power is absolute, thoughtful of detail, orderly, provident, and gentle. It would resemble parental authority if, fatherlike, it tried to prepare its charges for a man's life, but on the contrary, it only tries to keep them in perpetual childhood. It likes to see the citizens enjoy themselves, provided they think of nothing but enjoyment. It gladly works for their happiness but wants to be the sole agent and judge of it. It provides for their security, foresees and supplies their necessities, facilitates their pleasures, manages their principal concerns, directs their industry, makes rules for their testaments, and divides their inheritances. Why should it not entirely relieve them from the trouble of thinking and all the cares of living?[39]

Notes

1. Act of June 22, 1870; 16 Statutes at Large 162.
2. Act of September 24, 1789; 1 Statutes at Large 92–3.
3. Aristotle, *Nicomachean Ethics*, Book 5, 1130a15–1132b19.
4. Ibid., 1132a3–9.
5. Thomas Hobbes, *Leviathan*, Part 1, chap. 15, Michael Oakeshott, ed. (Oxford: Basil Blackwell, n.d.), p. 98.
6. Aristotle, *Nicomachean Ethics*, Book 5, 1130b32–1131a2.
7. Hobbes, *Leviathan*, p. 98.
8. Ibid.
9. Alexander Hamilton, James Madison, and John Jay, *The Federalist Papers*, No. 8, ed. Clinton Rossiter (New York: New American Library, 1961), p. 69.

10. *Selective Service Draft Law Cases*, 245 U.S. 366 (1918); Welsh v. United States, 398 U.S. 333 (1970); Selective Service System v. Minnesota Public Interest Research Group, 468 U.S. 841 (1984); *Hearings before the Select Committee on Intelligence of the United States Senate*, 96th Congress, 2d sess., on Intelligence Identities Protective Legislation, June 24, 25, 1980 (Washington, D.C.: Government Printing Office, 1980), p. 89.

The point made in the text has to be balanced by mention of the fact that in times of danger, and sometimes even of imaginary danger, the public authorities are sometimes inclined to take an expanded view of the "permanent and aggregate interests of the community." In the most egregious case, they will insist that the public safety requires the relocation and detention of an entire class of persons, some of them native-born citizens and none of them convicted of a criminal offense. See Korematsu v. United States, 323 U.S. 214 (1944).

The task of defining the line between these realms—private rights and public interest or necessity—has been given to the judiciary, ultimately to the Supreme Court; its duty is to serve as an arbiter of commutative justice in Hobbes's sense. But, as the Korematsu case illustrates, the Court does not always do well. As I said, establishing this justice is not a simple matter.

11. John Locke, *Two Treatises of Government*, II, secs. 34, 123, and 21.

12. Madison repeats this point in *Federalist* 51 and in the process reveals his indebtedness to Locke:

Justice [he writes] is the end of government. It is the end of civil society. It ever has been and ever will be pursued until it be obtained, or until liberty be lost in the pursuit. In a society under the forms of which the stronger faction can readily unite and oppress the weaker, anarchy may as truly be said to reign as in a state of nature, where the weaker individual is not secured against the violence of the stronger; and as, in the latter state, even the stronger individuals are prompted, by the uncertainty of their condition, to submit to a government which may protect the weak as well as themselves; so, in the former state, will the more powerful factions or parties be gradually induced, by a like motive, to wish for a government which will protect all parties, the weaker as well as the more powerful.

13. Locke, *Treatises*, I, secs. 88, 89.

14. Madison, *Federalist* 10.

15. Jean-Jacques Rousseau, *Discourse on the Origin and Foundations of Inequality*, in Roger D. Masters, ed., *The First and Second Discourses* (New York: St. Martin's Press, 1964), p. 174.

16. Alexis de Tocqueville, *Democracy in America*, vol. 1, part 2, chap. 6, trans. George Lawrence (New York: Doubleday, Anchor Books, 1969), p. 238.

17. Max Farrand, ed., *The Records of the Federal Convention of 1787*, vol. 1 (New Haven, Conn.: Yale University Press, 1937), pp. 144, 534, 469–70, 533, 428.

18. Ibid., pp. 150 and 153.

19. Ibid., p. 152.

20. Tocqueville, *Democracy in America*, p. 238.

21. Abraham Lincoln, "Message to Congress in Special Session, July 4, 1861," in *The Collected Works of Abraham Lincoln,* vol. 4, ed. Roy P. Basler (New Brunswick, N.J.: Rutgers University Press, 1953), p. 438.

22. Nathan Tarcov, "American Constitutionalism and Individual Rights," in Robert A. Goldwin and William A. Schambra, eds., *How Does the Constitution Secure Rights?* (Washington, D.C.: American Enterprise Institute, 1985), p. 118.

23. Constitution of the USSR, 1936, Article 118.

24. George Wilson Pierson, *Tocqueville and Beaumont in America* (New York: Oxford University Press, 1938), p. 70.

25. *Federalist* 51.

26. Pierson, *Tocqueville and Beaumont,* p. 115.

27. Thomas Jefferson, *Notes on the State of Virginia* (New York: Harper Torchbook, 1964), Query vi, pp. 55–64; Query x, p. 90; app. 1, p. 184.

28. Ibid., Query xiv, p. 138.

29. Ibid., Query xviii, p. 155.

30. Jefferson, "Autobiography," in Adrienne Koch and William Peden, eds., *The Life and Selected Writings of Thomas Jefferson* (New York: Modern Library, 1944), p. 51.

31. See Walter Berns, *Taking the Constitution Seriously* (New York: Simon and Schuster, 1987), chap. 1.

32. Thornburg v. Gingles, 106 S.Ct. 2752, 2785 (1986), concurring opinion.

33. Goldberg v. Kelly, 397 U.S. 254 (1970).

34. R. Shep Melnick, "Judicial Activism Meets the New Congress: The Growth of Programmatic Rights" (Paper presented at Harvard University, March 1987), p. 28 note.

35. Johnson v. Transportation Agency, Santa Clara County, California, 107 S.Ct. 1442, 1467 (1987), dissenting opinion. The statute involved is Title VII of the Civil Rights Act of 1964, 42 U.S.C. sec. 2000e–2(a).

36. Tocqueville, *Democracy in America,* vol. 1, Author's Introduction, p. 12.

37. See, generally, John Rawls, *A Theory of Justice* (Cambridge, Mass.: Harvard University Press, 1971).

38. Ronald Dworkin, *Taking Rights Seriously* (Cambridge, Mass.: Harvard University Press, 1977), pp. 149, 206–22, 266–78.

39. Tocqueville, *Democracy in America,* vol. 2, part 4, chap. 6, p. 692.

4

Reconciling Different Views about Constitutional Interpretation

Henry G. Manne

Recent years have witnessed the development of a truly historic debate about the nature of constitutional law in the United States, particularly the role of the U.S. Supreme Court in the interpretation of the Constitution. This debate has raged in academic circles, among distinguished jurists and government officials, and at most every level of public concern.

The Contending Positions

The issue is undeniably affected by normative preferences for the results given by one position or another. It would be a serious mistake, however, to allow the debate to be resolved on that ground. The criticism of the famous, or infamous, case of *Roe* v. *Wade* on purely methodological and interpretative grounds should not be confounded with one's attitude toward the underlying subject of abortion. Similarly, the Supreme Court's failure for many years to protect property interests should be addressed in terms of the intrepretational craftsmanship and constitutional propriety of these rulings, not in terms of political attitudes about government regulation or government's taking possession of private property.

Without such a "positive" approach to the subject, arguments about how the Constitution should be interpreted cannot and should not be taken seriously. That is not to say that there are not serious questions about the morality of abortion or the desirability of private property; there is, however, an issue of constitutional interpretation that for present purposes must be allowed to transcend the results in particular cases. At the same time, the mere fact that advocates in this debate do have their own underlying policy preferences should not detract from the validity that may be found in their arguments. A system of advocacy where each side has a normative or selfish interest may still best advance the debate, as it generally does in our system of litigation. Ultimately, though, the correct current debate is about methodology, not political preferences.

The burden of persuasion has been assumed in recent years by the so-called interpretivists, the advocates of an original intent jurisprudence. Most notable among the spokesmen for this position have been former Attorney General Edwin Meese and ex-Judge Robert Bork. They are, of course, only the most recent in a long and distinguished line of proponents of one form or another of this approach. Indeed, it is fair to say that until no more than twenty-five years ago, there was no serious alternative to an interpretivist position, and the Supreme Court has paid lip service, if not always strict deference, to this position.

It will be helpful for present purposes, therefore, to review the fundamental arguments in favor of an original intent constitutional jurisprudence. That will be followed in turn by a discussion of various arguments against this position and finally by arguments pro and con for the noninterpretivists' position, now most popularly advocated by Justice William Brennan and Professor Laurence Tribe.

Strongly supporting an original intent approach is the common sense observation that our constitutional law seems to have no logical basis apart from what was expressed in the document by the founders. This argument, in turn, can be elaborated in several ways. First of all, the Constitution can be seen as the embodiment of a social contract, and social contracts must be observed until, in the course of events, they are amended or overthrown by revolution. Any change short of one resulting from amendment or revolution would seem to involve an abuse of authority by an interpreting agency, in this case the U.S. Supreme Court. Adoption of a written constitution by the United States of America probably did more to popularize the "social compact" theory of government than any other single event in the history of Western policy thought. This is a deeply sensed, almost sacred aspect of our political tradition and one that can arguably be observed properly only by strict regard for the intent of the draftsmen.

A related argument is that the very purpose of having a written constitution is to provide an exclusive framework within which the intention of the founders can be discovered. We were not handed down a broad, Decalogue-like statement of principle; rather, we were handed down a constitution that in many respects is quite specific and detailed. The very existence of those specific provisions argues in favor of some interpretivist position, since one would not normally assume that different philosophical or methodological approaches to

56

the same document were appropriate when (or because) some areas were spelled out in detail while others were not. Yet no one questions our following the "original intent" or the "plain meaning" on, for instance, the age required to be a president. While drafting deficiencies, omissions, and generalizations do imply some judicial discretion when new and uncontemplated situations arise, that certainly does not necessarily mandate an evolving set of constitutional standards. A written document still provides the compass bearing by which judicial navigators should find their way.

A related point is that, unless the Supreme Court closely ties its interpretations to the intent of the founders as revealed in the document, there is no effective constraint against abuse of authority by the Court itself. Far from being the "least dangerous branch" of the government, the federal court system can be, and some would argue already has been, converted into an uncontrolled producer of new policy initiatives without even the political inhibition of periodic elections. It would be more than passing strange if the Founding Fathers ever intended to create a Supreme Court with this kind of potential for arbitrary lawmaking. Even proponents of a noninterpretivist view really do not claim that the Court is entitled to be an unconstrained and lawless agency of government, only that a preference for a kind of floating constitutional interpretation must now be attributed to the founders.

A related argument is also persuasive. Judicial review (the type of which is the subject of the modern debate) is nowhere mentioned in the Constitution. Its justification is strongly premised on the view that without it the explicit limitations on congressional and presidential powers would be meaningless or useless. It would be an odd constitution, however, that implied the power of the judiciary to enforce limitations on the other branches and then allowed no effective limitation on the judiciary itself. If judicial review is to be assumed, given the judiciary's potential for abuse, then it must also be assumed that some limitation on this power too is an appropriate inference of the founders' intent. Some form of original intent argument is probably a necessary concomitant of the very idea of judicial review.

A final argument in favor of the original intent position is a purely practical response to the charge that the Court must be accorded flexibility in dealing with new situations and attitudes, a favorite noninterpretivist position. The answer is simply that changes in the Constitution can be made through the amendment process and that this is the method that has been used historically when even the grossest changes in the previous rules were dictated. Certainly the Civil War determined that slavery would no longer be tolerated as a constitutional matter but that evil and some of its political progeny (the Emancipation Proclamation aside) were dealt with through the post–Civil War amendments.

There are, however, significant arguments against various forms of the original intent position—not the least of these proceeds from modern public choice scholarship. That demonstrates, more clearly than was previously understood, that the concept of a "group intent" is merely a theoretical construct, not a reflection of an objective reality, when there is no strict unanimity of preference among members of a group. Indeed, unanimity did not exist in 1787 or 1789, or there would have been no occasion for compromises or general and abstract terms (for example, "due process"). The group intent argument of the interpretivists often implies that constitutional holdings should reflect a post-mortem plebiscite of the Founding Fathers on the very questions they would not or could not answer. To the extent that modern interpretivist positions assume that there does exist a single real original intent on any question (and that it can be gleaned from written words or from any other evidence), the argument lacks intellectual plausibility.

Interpretivists might respond that the document, not some objective intent of individuals, is really the proper basis for determining constitutional meaning. Thus the public choice criticism is largely muted, since whatever "intent" underlay the determination of the words of the document, once the document itself was written, we cannot seek intent from any source other than the words. The logic of this argument is closely akin to that of the parol evidence rule in standard contract law, that the parties' intent in a written contract must be found exclusively within the confines of the written words. No other evidence is admissible even for the purpose of resolving disputed interpretations.

Even this position, however, is no safe harbor for interpretivists. The search for meaning in the words of the document is no more reliable than other techniques for discovering original intent. The meanings of words are notoriously vague, ambiguous, and volatile; we could argue (and scholars have argued) endlessly about the nuances of meaning of the preposition *among* in eighteenth-century usage. Since the words of the document are so often unhelpful in answering hard, new constitutional questions, the reach of their meaning quickly becomes a function of the reader's subjective attitude or preference, clearly a noninterpretivist position.

For instance, some may read the First Amendment to be limited literally to "the press" and thus to provide little protection to the electronic media. Others may find the extension to modern communication systems an easy one, clearly including television within the constitutional meaning of "press." The debate over a constitutional right to privacy is beset by this same kind of interpretivist problem. It serves little end to complain huffily about one or the other of the positions when in fact it is not possible to state an objective standard for when a word or clause is to be defined narrowly and when it is to be read more generously.

Another fundamental argument against the original intent position (and central to the affirmative theory of this paper) is that while the purpose of the original intent approach is to preserve a degree of constancy in constitutional meaning through time, that is in fact impossible. The constancy or stability sought is in the underlying legal or governmental structure, not in the meaning of words themselves. And this structure cannot be preserved or stabilized solely by reference to the words of the document, since changes totally external to the constitutional system may substantially alter the real allocation of legal power without affecting the words at all.

Two illustrations may clarify this point. The Second Amendment to the Bill of Rights guarantees a citizen the right to "keep and bear arms." When these words were written, the muzzle-loaded musket was clearly the weapon the founders had in mind. Today, however, in the common vernacular "arms" includes automatic handguns and rifles, hand grenades, and perhaps even portable nuclear weapons, all available by the way to possibly intrusive governments. Quite clearly, as a result of these developments in weapons technology—all completely external to the Constitution—not even the strictest interpretivist would argue that a citizen's right to keep and bear arms was limited to the specific kind of arms the draftsmen had in mind. As soon as an interpretivist begins to talk about the modern equivalence of 1789 arms, however, he is no longer an interpretivist at all. And the more he uses "keep and bear arms" as a metaphor for self-protection, the more like a noninterpretivist he becomes. The undeniable fact is that a change in technology has drastically lessened the ability of citizens to defend themselves against modern armed intrusions. Whether we like it or not, the real constitution, that is the actual allocation of power as opposed to what is allegedly meant by the words in the legal document, has been altered by this change in technology. Thus it is difficult to see how a strict original intent, as gleaned from the document, can still lay claim to performing its most basic instrumental purpose, maintaining constitutional constancy.

There is another, even more dramatic illustration of this point. As a practical matter the enforcement reach of federal laws in 1787 was very short. Effective application of federal law was severely constrained by the primitive technologies of transportation and communications. For instance, it would have been utterly inconceivable and ludicrous for Congress to adopt a federal program for meat inspection in each of the original thirteen states. We can certainly conclude, therefore, that it was not a part of the intent of the founders that the federal government should have this kind of power. But the rapid development of communication and transportation technology through the nineteenth and twentieth centuries made physically possible a degree of federal law enforceability inconceivable in 1787. Federal meat inspection laws and the like are not only not constitutionally ludicrous, they flourish. So do we have the same Constitution today that we had then? Obviously not. The controlling words about interstate commerce are the same, but manifestly the reality is not.

While these arguments severely weaken the position of the interpretivists, they by no means carry the day for noninterpretivist positions. Indeed, every affirmative thrust ever offered to the "living Constitution" argument is an abject intellectual failure. This approach has no compelling logical, scientific, semantic, or even moral foundation. There is, in a word, nothing objective about it. No amount of emoting about the *Zeitgeist*, natural rights, or human dignity can alter the fact that the usual noninterpretivist position states a claim for a special degree of authority for one branch of the federal government, the judiciary. It is an argument based peculiarly on the moral confidence its advocates seem to have in their own ideological positions, whether this be liberal, conservative, or libertarian.

Two arguments against the noninterpretivists' position should be part of the public debate, although they normally are not. The first of these is that the argument for a living constitution, one that evokes new rights and constraints primarily from inexplicit principles of the Constitution (whether historical or semantic in origin), greatly politicizes the process of constitutional litigation. This necessarily follows from the implicit ideological basis of the arguments. The original intent argument, at least to the extent that people have confidence in the integrity of the judges applying it, logically admits of no such popular debate. A Supreme Court that professes to apply the original intent approach may be criticized because of errors of method or of craftsmanship but not because the general polity does not like the result. Under such a regime the recourse must necessarily be to the legislative or to the amendment process. It is conducive to the preservation of the republic for constitutional issues to be seen as legal questions, not as policy issues to be democratically or politically addressed.

The current debate about *Roe* v. *Wade*, perhaps the epitome of noninterpretivist Supreme Court constitutional opinion, illustrates this point. Lobbies and policy-oriented groups addressing this legal topic argue primarily about the desirability or the undesirability of abortions, not about the propriety or lack thereof in discovering a constitutional right to abortion. The opinion that was written invites just such a "political" response; the public was educated by the Court's opinion to argue about this matter based on their approval or disapproval of abortions and not on whether the opinion reflected a desirable or an undesirable approach to constitutional adjudications. This case would not have been so socially divisive if the Supreme Court had shown greater respect for legal craftsmanship and traditional style in formulating its opinion.

A closely related point is that the noninterpretivist position greatly politicizes the appointments process. Rarely in history has this been more dramatically demonstrated than in connection with President Ronald Reagan's nomination of Judge Robert Bork to the Supreme Court. The country endured an unseemly political-style campaign impugning the nominee's attitudes on abortion, capital punishment, a free press, welfare, civil rights, economic regulation, and the like. In fact, however, the nominee's personal moral, economic, or social preferences in these matters should, under any reasonable premise about a rule of law, be of importance only if it could first be demonstrated that he would fail a test of technical competence, a matter not even intimated by Judge Bork's strongest opponents. By making each constitutional issue a matter of social, moral, or economic policy and not a matter of constitutional interpretation as such, the noninterpretivists force us to measure the political significance and acceptability of each appointment, rather than the nominee's competence and integrity. Surely the dangers of this approach transcend current political differences between conservatives and liberals. A politicized appointments process makes a mockery of the notion of appointing rather than electing federal judges. Again it is hard to imagine a more socially divisive element in any constitutional democracy.

A Peculiar Debate

Those who have followed the intricacies of the current constitutional debate, and the criticisms presented here, may have noticed a most peculiar matter. While there is substantial, indeed almost conclusive, force to the *negative* arguments made on each side of the debate, there is little if any merit to the positive ones. "Intent" cannot be found or preserved, and a "living" constitution in effect is no constitution at all. Yet such is the state of the current debate that each side implicitly demands that we choose one of these approaches. In fact, there may be an alternative, an approach that can claim some of the advantages of either approach with none of the debilitating weaknesses, though, to be sure, it has its own problems. Before an introduction to the new approach, it may be useful to notice a special characteristic that interpretivists and noninterpretivists share.

Each side purports to offer a better way *to interpret the constitutional document.* And this focus on the document itself may provide a clue about why each side has gone wrong. Much of the problem may stem from what might be called "lawyers' conceit." That is, in the matter of interpreting the Constitution, even when viewed by parties as dissimilar in their policy orientations as Justice Brennan and Attorney General Meese, there is implicit agreement that the work must be done only as lawyers would do it. The proponents generally agree that the matter is essentially one of documentary interpretation and that that is lawyers' work par excellence.

Shocking though it will sound to most lawyers, however, we are not required to begin our study of the Constitution with the document itself. There is no parol evidence rule that prevents us from understanding the relevant prehistory of the Constitution, nor a rule that binds us to interpret the Constitution as we would a lease of a partnership agreement. We, as the progeny of the Founding Fathers, are not bound in the same way that modern judges in commercial or real estate matters are bound by standard rules regarding written documents. The Founding Fathers, unlike negotiating attorneys today, were not interested in producing a document as an end in itself. Rather they were interested in creating a governmental system or structure, with defined relationships between the parts, that would promote liberty and welfare. As we shall see, there is a world of difference between these two approaches. Yet the superficial similarity of our Constitution to commonplace legal documents has for too long distorted our common sense about how we should deal with constitutional questions.

In a relatively "nonlegalistic" approach to constitutional interpretation, certain other matters should also be noted. This is not an argument about the "structure of government" as that phrase is usually used. In much modern political science literature a view called "structuralist" is used to denote the individual role or function of the various components of the government established by the Constitution. The focus is on the Supreme Court, the Congress, the states, the president, the cabinet, and so forth, each viewed as a kind of peculiar political entity, each with its own authority and limitations as described in the Constitution. We do not hear much about this approach in the modern debate about interpretation for the obvious reason that it says almost nothing about how the Constitution should be interpreted. A strict structural approach to understanding the American system of government carries no implications for how we are to move beyond its static descriptions.

A closely related point, popularized by John Hart Ely, is that the Constitution is aimed not so much toward substantive structural ends as toward process and procedure. This approach, unlike the usual structural argument, does contain implications for interpretation. Ely has developed the notion that in interpreting the Constitution, the Supreme Court is bound to protect democratic participatory rights of minorities. This approach, however, merely provides us with a policy goal (a form of participatory democracy) with which Supreme Court opinions should be consistent. In this sense it is too limited. While it seems to offer an explanation, or perhaps a rationalization, for the development of some modern civil rights law, it offers little help in matters relating, for example, to protection of property rights or to the power of Congress to participate in foreign policy.

Another word of caution is called for here. Some writers have suggested that the framers were designing a "libertarian" political structure to prevent the dominance of "special interests" in legislatures. Under this view constitutional issues should be decided consistently with the ideals of private property and open markets. Whether one likes this view or not, though, it is merely another noninterpretivist argument and fails for the usual reasons. In this paper references to contending "entities" or structural parts do not refer to the notion of competing "special interests" or pressure groups. Our concern here is not with groups lobbying legislatures for monopoly privileges or, in modern public choice terms, engaged in "rent seeking." Thus it is not a part of this theory to invite the courts to evaluate the propriety of political deals, as some writers have suggested, or to apply libertarian ideology as the goal of judicial review. Rent seeking was a matter of fact in 1787 and 1789 just as it is in 1988, but its growing claim to theoretical significance in the modern literature of political economy should no more be allowed to change our real constitution than did the development of railroads.

A Reconciliation

In our effort to deemphasize the document, we might perhaps begin with a directly alternative formulation: that is, that the Founding Fathers should be seen as creating not a document but a governmental structure composed of dynamically competing and interacting political parts. This would include citizens as important actors in the total complex structure since they, like other components, would from time to time be in conflict with the other parts, thereby giving rise to constitutional issues. In addressing conflicts between components, specific, explicit powers granted by the document would only rarely be helpful. Rather than concentrate on the explicit power or rights granted to any specific component, as might be done by an interpretivist, our interest should be on the *relative* power positions of the two conflicting components. That is, the major significance of any power grant or limitation in the Constitution does not lie in its explicit declaration in a vacuum (for example, the president's command of the armed forces) but rather in its intended power position relative to other constitutional components. What was most likely intended—or at least what we would do well to infer today—was that these *same relative positions or proportions* should be preserved. Only with that approach can a notion of original intent serve as a logical basis for judicial review.

The critical touchstone then of this approach is neither to interpret words nor to apply normative principles. It is rather the less dramatic but more logical goal of preserving a constant ratio of power between any two components of the constitutional structure. Thus, for example, it is far less important that the Constitution state that certain aspects of foreign policy should be executed solely by the president than that this provision be understood as one of several determining a certain ratio of power between the president and the Congress (as the other relevant entity in this case). Only that ratio of power, or proportion, could the Founding Fathers be reasonably assumed to have wanted to keep constant, not the absolute value of either the numerator (the president's authority) or the denominator (Congress's powers) in the ratio as a rule of strict interpretation would imply.

Probably no other area of current constitutional debate more dramatically or clearly demonstrates how changes (not all technological) exogenous to the Constitution can clearly affect the real allocation of power. In 1787 the founders certainly realized that Congress's role in the budget process would be a restraint on the president's powers in foreign affairs. The force of that restraint in 1787, however, was in turn limited by the relative unimportance of budgetary matters to foreign policy. In 1787 budgets played a small part, both because of the limited role of the United States in foreign affairs and because of the relative insignificance of finances in our foreign affairs. We see what has happened now, however. Over a third of our total budget goes for defense and aspects of foreign relations. The role of

Congress as a result has grown enormously over what it was in George Washington's time, although without an amendment to the Constitution. Surely to continue to interpret Congress's and the president's foreign powers purely in terms of the explicit delegations (foreign affairs and budgetary) of the Constitution is a recipe for unwarranted and random constitutional change.

This insight still leaves a major practical weakness, however: it is very difficult to measure the relative power of political components in a useful fashion.

It would be desirable if we had a clear metric to represent the cardinal amount (other than zero and infinity) of actual power given to a particular part of the government structure, including citizens. Then, as new exogenous events occur to shift that measure of real power either upward or downward, we could have a base from which to count. We do not have such a metric, but *neither do either of the contending theories,* even though they imply that the Court will be able to identify some objective limit beyond which any stated power is to be limited. That is merely another way of stating that anything beyond a certain cardinal limit is unconstitutional. Neither interpretivists nor noninterpretivists, however, have any objective method of specifying that boundary, and that weakness in the "structural ratio" approach should no more be controlling here than it is elsewhere.

In fact, we should not expect the law to be amenable to precise measurement. If that were available, a mechanical process could replace politics, government, and law. Part of our law's genius has been its ability to address implicitly quantitative issues in a qualitative fashion. That is required in this instance too, and the absence of a cardinal metric is not a sufficient basis for rejecting this approach.

We can function, if we are concerned about a ratio of powers, without a clear numerical measure of specific changes in the effective constitutional power of a component. We need only to understand gross relative positions, a function well within the powers of our legal system.

If we may finesse further discussion of this difficult measurement issue, we can turn to the underlying jurisprudential role of the federal courts in maintaining constitutional constancy or structural ratio equilibrium. As we have seen, exogenous events may lead to important changes in the original constitutional equilibrium. The fact that exogenous forces may push the "value" or weight of one component far in one direction with no offsetting change in a competing component, however, need not result in the Constitution's being permanently altered thereby. The Supreme Court would have the authority—and under this view the duty—to reestablish the *original equilibrium ratio,*

65

even though the Court can do nothing about the external event that brought about the change in the value of one of the two competing variables.

An example may serve to make this clearer. When the draftsmen wrote the Constitution, we can assume that they had decided upon certain relative positions of Congress and state legislatures vis-à-vis the regulation of commerce. The language of the Constitution giving Congress power to regulate "commerce among the several states" is familiar albeit not explicitly clear. In 1787, though, the idea that the federal government could effectively regulate matters relating, for example, to coal mine safety standards would have seemed absurd, not merely as a legal matter but, much more important, as a practical matter. It was not physically possible for the federal government to serve its writ widely enough to allow it effective authority over every detail of all commercial matters. That could, however, be comprehended as within the states' area of responsibility, and so it was.

Then several things happened to change this matter of technical or administrative feasibility. Railroads developed, and a little later the wire telegraph appeared. Even later enormous systems of roads, telephones, radio, television, airplanes, and computers appeared. Now the physical or technological task of reaching into every nook and cranny of the entire nation became mere child's play. As a result a gross alteration of the federal government's physical power to regulate commerce had occurred. Yet when the courts looked to the words of the document and to the "original intent," we know from past history exactly what happened. The legal concept of interstate commerce grew *pari passu* with the federal government's ability to administer laws locally. While the words did not change, the Supreme Court allowed the constant expansion of federal regulatory powers in keeping with the changes in markets and market structure occasioned by the new technology. They could find no significant explicit limitation on Congress's interstate commerce power because there was no real objective boundary in the document, only words.

What had actually happened to change our constitutional reality in this drastic fashion? Had there been an amendment or a revolution? No, there had been only the invention or introduction of new technologies by nonelected scientists and entrepreneurs.

This realistic scenario depicts a world in which the actual allocation of constitutional authority can be dramatically altered by developments and events totally outside the political process. In other words, the accidents of technological development determine the real limits on the restraining influence of the Constitution. The same can be shown for wars, organizational innovations, demographic changes, international developments, scientific discoveries, and undoubtedly other matters (but not including changes in social or moral attitudes) not normally contemplated as effecting changes in the Constitution.

What a bizarre system, a constitutional lottery where constitutional authority is given and taken for reasons and by forces that have absolutely nothing to do with the desirability or undesirability of the result, that are in no sense democratic, and whose political consequences will tend to be ratcheted quickly into permanence! Yet neither side in the current debate has identified or provided any solution to this problem. Neither strict construction of the document nor appeal to the *Zeitgeist* or constitutional penumbras can successfully cope with the impact on the actual boundaries of constitutional authority resulting from exogenous developments.

Once we understand the problem of arbitrarily occurring constitutional change, however, a remedy may be at hand. Manifestly it is not to try to control the external variables, such as suggestions once heard to restrain the use of computers because they threatened privacy. Nor should the Court merely tolerate the change, as it has in the past, because a semantic standard was not violated. The solution is for the Supreme Court of the United States to assume a responsibility for reestablishing constitutional equilibrium after a significant unintended change has occurred. Its role would be something akin to that of an automatic pilot that returns the ship of state to its original course after unanticipated winds have blown it off course.

Thus as the Court (informed perhaps as much by history and political theory as by legalisms) recognizes that events, for whatever reason, have shifted the ratio of power too far in one direction to be consistent with the original prescribed proportion, its primary responsibility is to reestablish the intended equilibrium. This can be done either by restricting the already expanded authority or by expanding the other variable. Exactly how that will be done is a matter of statesmanship, legal craftsmanship, and discretion that we must perforce leave to the courts. But at least the assigned task (difficult as it may be in practice) makes sense, and that should help the courts understand and fulfill their proper role in preserving the constitutional framework. The notion of ratios of power in this connection will undoubtedly sound strange to many. It is not a concept that appears in the traditional constitutional literature. Two such ratios have been suggested above, one the relationship between Congress and the president on matters of foreign policy and the other the ratio between the federal government (here Congress) and the states on matters of commercial regulation. That is just a sample, though, of what can be an enormous list.

Every single component of the constitutional system contemplated by the Founding Fathers must be included. The list would include citizens of the United States; citizens of the states; aliens; convicted criminals; defendants in criminal cases; citizens in the performance of various protected activities, such as religion, speech, and the like; the Congress of the United States; administrative agencies; the Supreme Court; the cabinet; the president of the United States; lower federal courts; states; the armed forces; juries; and undoubtedly others. This listing of components just begins to describe the task, for each set of two components might then comprehend numerous constitutionally significant subject areas. Thus, as between Congress and citizens, these would be a variety of matters indicated in the Bill of Rights. As between the president and Congress, for instance, there would be issues relating to the conduct of foreign affairs, administrative regulation, and executive privilege. No effort will be made to list here all the constitutional issues that could be addressed with a structural ratio approach. The list would comprehend every aspect of constitutional conflict.

The matter is even more complicated than might first appear because the Court, in assessing the proper relative power of one component vis-à-vis another, must also take into account the effects on other ratios not directly involved in the litigation at hand. Thus the Court might want to resolve a disequilibrium in the ratio of regulatory powers of Congress and of the states by increasing the power of the states. This in turn, though, might too strongly deny an individual's property rights. In that event the Court would have no choice but to limit Congress's powers and not to enlarge the states'. The point is that it is a complex constitutional structure that is being preserved, not simple ratios taken in a vacuum.

The structural ratio approach still does not—and is not necessarily intended to—provide an easy answer to specific constitutional cases, particularly many recent ones that have received great attention. In fact, by its nature this approach would have the salutary effect of greatly reducing the number of significant constitutional holdings. Precedent, of the usual common law variety, should play its customary role of "developing" or elaborating legal doctrine—at least until the appropriate time arrived for constitutional redirection. Precedent, then, would allow the courts to temporize until a structural ratio had gotten so far out of line as to dictate a judicial nudge back toward the intended equilibrium. In other words, a "straying off course" of a line of cases could at some point be tantamount to an external change affecting the constitutional balance. The Supreme Court, however, would decide cases just as any court does until a constitutional correction became necessary.

Important constitutional opinions should articulate the best knowledge about what relationship the founders were actually trying to establish between the competing units, how external variables have changed or threaten to change the intended power ratio, and finally how the Court will reestablish the prior equilibrium. This approach is so unlike anything the Court has ever done that much more study is required before we can suggest actual techniques. At this point, all that can be confidently proposed is the underlying logic of the approach, not the details of technique and application. If the underlying logic is correct, the modes of detailed analysis should eventually evolve.

Conclusion

All the strong arguments favoring an original intent approach to constitutional interpretation are incorporated into the structural ratio approach—with one enormous difference. We are no longer plagued by the problems of group intent or of semantic confusions. The powers actually intended can now be preserved in spite of external changes that would otherwise randomly alter constitutional powers. A focus on the structure of the government created in 1787 and 1789 rather than on the words used in the document will help resolve disagreements in a way that existing opinions, not based on a positive methodology, do not.

The major problem with the structural ratio approach is application, not theory. For instance, as noted, it is probably impossible to quantify the relative powers of competing components of a political system accurately. We do not have such a metric. Still, a court could probably develop impressionistic measures using verbal standards. The law is full of such "measurements," such as "preponderance of the evidence," "due process," or "beyond a reasonable doubt." The important matter will be to articulate some standard description of the comparative powers as seen by the Founding Fathers. Once this ratio is wholly defined, the Court still must determine whether one part of the ratio has become skewed, and then it must decide on the most appropriate means for reestablishing the original ratio.

This idea needs to be developed and refined by scholars in a variety of fields, including law. It presents an invitation to historians, political scientists, theologians, scientists, and others to participate as equals in a debate that should concern all classes of citizens. Indeed, if we do not steer the constitutional interpretation debate away from policy-oriented methodologies, we face the grave danger of losing the idea of a regime of law altogether.

5

"Interpreting" the Constitution

Michael J. Perry

Everyone agrees that courts should resolve constitutional conflicts on the basis of the Constitution and that therefore the courts should and even must interpret the Constitution. But there is widespread disagreement about what it means to "interpret" the Constitution.

On one side of the controversy are the "originalists"—people like Chief Justice William Rehnquist, Judge Robert Bork, and Attorney General Edwin Meese. They argue that the Constitution ought to mean *no more* today than it meant in the past and that to interpret the Constitution, therefore, is simply to uncover its *original* meaning.

On the other side of the controversy are the "nonoriginalists"—Justice William Brennan is a prominent example. They argue that, fortunately, the Constitution often means *more* today than it meant in the past and that to interpret the Constitution, therefore, is to discern its *present* meaning.

Originalists like Chief Justice Rehnquist want the courts to retreat to the relatively small role of uncovering and enforcing the *narrow* original meaning of the Constitution. Nonoriginalists, by contrast, understand that it is important that the courts maintain the larger role of discerning and enforcing the *broad* present meaning of the Constitution.

This debate is not an abstract conversation in academic political theory. The future of our constitutional rights and liberties—and of the courts' role in protecting them—is at stake: The original meaning of the Constitution does not support a generous understanding of our constitutional rights and liberties, because the original meaning is narrow. A generous understanding of our constitutional rights and liberties requires the present meaning of the (various relevant provisions of the) Constitution, which is broader than the original meaning.

Editors' note: Although AEI style follows the long-established practice of using masculine pronouns for general references, feminine pronouns are used throughout this paper at the insistence of the author.

The following reflections, drawn from a much longer work, are intended to clarify the debate and to present and defend aspects of the nonoriginalist position.[1]

Authority and Symbol

In American political-legal culture it is axiomatic that the Constitution is authoritative—indeed, supremely authoritative—in constitutional adjudication. That is, it is axiomatic that constitutional cases should be decided on the basis of, according to, the Constitution. (Similarly, in American political-legal culture "the law" is axiomatically authoritative in adjudication: it is axiomatic that judges should decide cases "according to law.") It is *not* axiomatic, however, what it means to say that the Constitution is authoritative, because, as I will explain, it is not axiomatic what, precisely, "the Constitution" means or, therefore, is. (Similarly, it is not axiomatic what it means to say that judges should decide cases according to law, because it is not axiomatic what "the law" means or, therefore, is.) According to originalism, what does it mean to say that the Constitution is authoritative? And what does it mean to interpret the Constitution, according to orginalism? What does it mean to say that the Constitution is authoritative—and what does it mean to interpret the Constitution—according to non-originalism?

Our Constitution is written. Our Constitution is a text. To say that something (for example, marks on a page) is a text (and not just marks on a page) is to conclude that that something is meaningful—that is, meaning-ful, full of meaning. For a person to say that something is a text when that something is not (yet) meaningful to her—perhaps because it is written in a language or code she does not (yet) understand—is for her to conclude, perhaps only tentatively, that that something is a text for someone, that it is, potentially at least, meaningful to someone, perhaps even (potentially) to her.

For the originalist the meaning of the constitutional text is *the original meaning;* to enforce the Constitution is to enforce it *as originally understood* (by the ratifiers or the framers and ratifiers). For originalism, then, to interpret the Constitution is to ascertain the original meaning—the beliefs the text was originally understood to signify—and then to answer the question what significance, if any, those beliefs have for the conflict at hand, what those beliefs, if accepted, require the court to do, if anything, with respect to the conflict at hand. Thus for originalism the interpretation of a constitutional provision comprises two interpretive moments: a moment in which the original meaning or understanding of the provision is ascertained (to

71

the extent possible) and a second moment in which the significance of that meaning for the conflict at hand is ascertained.

For the nonoriginalist, too, of course, the constitutional text is meaning-ful. But for the nonoriginalist the meaning of the text is not singular. *One* meaning of the constitutional text is the original meaning. But for the nonoriginalist that is not the only meaning of the text.

A text can have multiple meanings. (Indeed, one meaning of a text can contradict another meaning of the text.) Meaning is always meaning to someone, and what a text means to one person is not necessarily what it means to another. But is it the case that a text can have more than one meaning to a person? Yes, to the extent that the text is more than one thing to her. To some persons, myself included, the constitutional text in certain of its aspects is more than one thing: it is a communication to us (the present) from the ratifiers and framers (the past), and, in virtue of a role it has come to play in the life of our political community—a role not necessarily foreseen much less authorized by any group of ratifiers and framers—it is *also* a symbol of fundamental aspirations of the political tradition. (Although a person is imaginable to whom the constitutional text is only a symbol and not also a communication from the ratifiers and framers, I doubt that in reality there are many such persons.) Thus, were someone to ask me what the equal protection clause means, I might say: "As a communication to us from the ratifiers and framers of the Fourteenth Amendment, it means . . . As a symbol of a fundamental aspiration of our political tradition, however, it means . . ." There is, after all, no rule that a text must be one and only one thing to a person—or, therefore, that it must mean one and only one thing to a person. Things are not so simple. Like some other texts (like every other text?), the constitutional text is polysemous.

For the nonoriginalist, unlike the originalist, some provisions of the constitutional text have a meaning *in addition to* the original meaning: some provisions are *symbolic of fundamental aspirations of the American political tradition.* Not every provision of the text is symbolic of such aspirations, but some are. The least controversial examples of such provisions are probably the First Amendment, symbolizing the tradition's aspirations to the freedoms of speech, the press, and religion; the Fifth Amendment, symbolizing the aspiration to due process of law; and the Fourteenth Amendment, symbolizing the aspirations to due process of law and to equal protection of the laws.

It seems invariably (though not necessarily) the case that the symbolic meaning of a constitutional provision, like the free speech clause of the First Amendment, has grown out of the original meaning. The symbolic meaning has emerged over time—in the course of adjudication and even of political discourse—as a progressive generalization of the original meaning. Thus the broad symbolic meaning is not inconsistent with but indeed includes the narrow original meaning.

Whether a particular provision is symbolic can be controversial, of course. To say that a particular provision is not symbolic of a fundamental aspiration of the American political tradition is to say either or both of two things: (1) that the provision does not function as a symbol; (2) that the aspiration the provision symbolizes is no longer a fundamental aspiration of the tradition.

Nonoriginalism does not hold that every fundamental aspiration of the tradition is necessarily symbolized by some provision of the text. Nor does it hold that every worthwhile aspiration is necessarily either (1) symbolized by some textual provision or even (2) a fundamental aspiration of the tradition. It does not even hold that every aspiration of the tradition symbolized by some textual provision is necessarily worthwhile.

Why should a judge bring to bear, in constitutional cases, *only* aspirations symbolized by the text? Why not all fundamental aspirations, even those not symbolized by the text? Indeed, why not all worthwhile aspirations, even those not fundamental aspirations of the American political tradition? If someone wants to claim that a judge should bring to bear all fundamental aspirations, or even all worthwhile aspirations, I want to hear the argument. (*Inter alia,* I am curious to hear what fundamental aspirations are not symbolized by the text and also what worthwhile aspirations are not fundamental aspirations of the tradition.) *My* argument is merely that a judge should bring to bear, in constitutional cases, only aspirations symbolized by the text.

Why should a judge bring those aspirations to bear? By oath a judge has sworn to support the Constitution. It is difficult to see what might be meant by "the Constitution" other than either (1) original beliefs or (2) the aspirations or ideals or principles symbolized by the Constitution. Given her oath, then, in adjudicating a case arising under a given textual provision, a judge's choice is either to pursue an originalist approach or, instead, to bring to bear the aspiration symbolized by the provision. My argument is that with respect to some provisions—those symbolizing fundamental aspirations of the American political tradition—she should forgo the originalist approach in favor of bringing the aspirations to bear.

Although I am arguing that a judge should bring to bear only aspirations symbolized by the Constitution (as distinct from all fundamental aspirations or all worthwhile aspirations), I am *not* arguing that she should bring to bear *every* aspiration symbolized by the Constitution. As I remarked a moment ago, nonoriginalism does not presuppose that every aspiration symbolized by the Constitution is necessarily worthwhile. If a judge believes that an aspiration symbolized by some provision of the constitutional text is not worthwhile, then she has no reason to bring that aspiration to bear. She may, consistently with her oath, pursue the originalist approach to adjudication under the provision in question. My discussion from this point forward assumes that the judge believes that the relevant aspiration *is* worthwhile and, therefore, that she *does* have reason to bring it to bear.

Originalists and nonoriginalists agree that the constitutional text is authoritative in constitutional adjudication, but they disagree about what it means to say that the text is authoritative. They disagree about that because they disagree about the meaning of the text. Whereas for the originalist the meaning of the constitutional text is singular—the meaning of the text is the original meaning—for the nonoriginalist the situation is more complicated. For reasons I give later, a nonoriginalist judge *is* interested in the original meaning of the Constitution; for her, too, one meaning of the text is the original meaning. But for a nonoriginalist judge that is not the text's only meaning. In a sense the originalist's Constitution is *not the same text*—it is *not meaningful in the same way*—as the nonoriginalist's Constitution (as least insofar as judicial review is concerned). For the originalist the constitutional text is authoritative in the sense that the original meaning is authoritative. For the nonoriginalist some provisions of the text are authoritative in the sense that their symbolic meaning—the aspirations they symbolize—is authoritative. For a nonoriginalist judge the authoritative meaning of some provisions of the constitutional text is not their narrow original meaning, but their broad symbolic meaning.

For nonoriginalism, then, to interpret some provisions of the Constitution is, in the main, to ascertain their symbolic meaning and then to bring that meaning to bear—that is, to answer the question what significance, if any, the aspiration symbolized by the relevant provision has for the conflict at hand, what that aspiration means for the conflict at hand, what that aspiration, if accepted, requires the court to do, if anything, with respect to the conflict at hand. Thus, for nonoriginalism no less than for originalism, the interpretation of a constitutional provision comprises two interpretive moments: a moment in which the symbolic meaning of the provision is ascertained and a second moment in which the significance of that meaning for the conflict at hand is ascertained. If, however, the symbolic meaning of a constitutional provision is readily apparent, then nonoriginalist interpretation of the provision will seem to involve only one interpretive moment: the moment in which the significance of the symbolic meaning for the conflict at hand is ascertained.

For both originalists and nonoriginalists, then, constitutional interpretation comprises two interpretive moments. Whereas the first moment yields a norm to be applied, the second moment—the moment of application—yields the significance of that norm for the conflict at hand. In the second moment the norm yielded in the first moment is specified, it is rendered more determinate. We might say that in the first moment the objective is the preliminary meaning of the constitutional provision and in the second moment the objective is the final meaning. Whereas the preliminary meaning is relatively general, abstract, formal, verbal, the final meaning is relatively particular, concrete, substantial, existential. For the originalist the proper objective for the first interpretive moment—that is, the proper preliminary meaning—is the original meaning. For the nonoriginalist, by contrast, it is the symbolic meaning.

Accountability and Justice

I now want to turn to the principal argument against the nonoriginalist conception of constitutional text, interpretation, and judicial role: "the argument from democracy," according to which nonoriginalism is illegitimate because undemocratic. What does it mean to say that nonoriginalism is undemocratic? And is it?

The value or ideal of electorally accountable policy making—the principle that governmental policy making (by which I mean simply decisions about which among competing values shall prevail and how those values shall be implemented) should be subject to control by persons accountable to the electorate—has an axiomatic or canonical status in American political-legal culture. But so do certain other values or aspirations, including those symbolized by certain provisions of the constitutional text. There is a deep and ineradicable tension in the American political tradition between the value of electorally accountable policy making and certain other values or ideals. As Robert McCloskey put it:

> Popular sovereignty suggests *will;* fundamental law suggests *limit.* The one idea conjures up the vision of an active, positive state; the other idea emphasizes the negative, restrictive side of the political problem. It may be possible to harmonize these seeming opposites by logical sleight of hand, by arguing that the doctrines of popular sovereignty and fundamental law were fused in the Constitution, which was a popularly willed limitation. But it seems unlikely that

Americans in general achieved such a synthesis and far more probable, considering our later political history, that most of them retained the two ideas side by side. This propensity to hold contradictory ideas simultaneously is one of the most significant qualities of the American political mind at all stages of national history, and it helps substantially in explaining the rise to power of the United States Supreme Court.[2]

Any conception of proper judicial role represents one way of embodying or institutionalizing the tension. No plausible conception—including the originalist—eradicates the tension. Any plausible conception compromises the value of electorally accountable policy making ("popular sovereignty") to some extent. A question for constitutional theory is, To what extent ought the value to be compromised, and in the service of what other values? (or, To what extent should the other values be compromised in the service of the value of electorally accountable policy making?).

In a previous book I made the mistake of assuming not merely that the value of electorally accountable policy making has an axiomatic status but that it is, as an axiom of American political-legal culture, lexically prior to all other values so that any conception of judicial role that compromises the value of electorally accountable policy making is illegitimate—or, at least, so that any conception of judicial role that compromises the value of electorally accountable policy making to a greater extent than another conception is inferior to that other conception.[3] Although the value of electorally accountable policy making *is* axiomatic in American political-legal culture, it is *not* axiomatic that that value is lexically prior to all other values. Justice Brennan has said that "faith in democracy is one thing, blind faith quite another." Americans have traditionally had faith in democracy but not blind faith. Consider, in that regard, this passage by Jack Rakove:

> The framers now most commonly appear as the perversely enlightened architects of the maddening obstacle course that has to be run every time a deserving piece of legislation is launched through a treacherous maze of congressional committees and executive agencies more worthy of a byzantine satrapy than the world's greatest democracy. In the view of such prominent political scientists as Robert Dahl and James MacGregor Burns, "the framers deliberately created a framework of government that was carefully designed to impede and even prevent the operation of majority rule." . . . Rather than look for ways to break the deadlock . . . [the framers] bequeathed, modern students of "The Founding" would

have us learn to appreciate the timeless concerns that led the framers to prevent government from becoming too vigorous for our own good. . . . In the influential formulation of Martin Diamond: "The reason of the Founders constructs the system within which the passions of the men who come after may be relied upon to operate in safely moderated channels."[4]

So, in evaluating the claim that nonoriginalism is "undemocratic," we must not assume that the value of electorally accountable policy making has an axiomatic priority over other fundamental values.

We must avoid as well the assumption that a particular conception of democracy, of how our governmental apparatus should be organized, is axiomatic for the American political tradition, so that the only question is whether the judicial role in question—here, the nonoriginalist role—is consistent with that axiomatic conception. That assumption will not do because the issue is precisely how our governmental apparatus should be organized. No particular conception of democracy—no particular conception of what the judicial role in that governmental apparatus should be—is axiomatic for the tradition. The tradition has never settled, even provisionally, on what the judicial role should be. That issue—unlike, say, the issue of whether blacks or women or eighteen-year-olds should be permitted to vote—has been and remains widely contested within the tradition.

The debate, properly understood, is about which conception of democracy should prevail. As Larry Alexander has emphasized, the constitutional-theoretical debate is "a dispute over what authority should be given to the political morality of present popular majorities, past and present Supreme Court justices, the various persons, committees, conventions, and legislatures associated with the framing of the Constitution, the words of the Constitution, and so forth."[5] Any particular conception of democracy, of what the judicial role should be within the overall governmental apparatus, must be defended. To presuppose the authoritative status of a particular conception is to beg the question. One must *argue for* a particular conception. (To argue for a particular conception of democracy, of judicial role within the governmental apparatus, is to argue for a particular conception of constitutional text and interpretation, namely, the conception entailed by the prescribed judicial role.) How do we conduct that argument—by reference to what considerations? How else but by reference to the ways in which a particular conception of judicial role comports with (or fails to comport with) the constitutive purposes and projects—the central aspirations—of the political tradition? A lot turns, therefore, on how one understands those central, constitutive aspirations.

One such aspiration, of course, is for governance that is both responsive and, because it is not always responsive, accountable to the electorate. Electorally accountable government is plainly not the only constitutive aspiration of the American political tradition, however. The tradition has aspired to "liberty and justice for all" as well as to "popular sovereignty." ("As we adapt our institutions to the ever-changing conditions of national and international life, . . . [the] ideals of human dignity—liberty and justice for all individuals—will continue to inspire and guide us because they are entrenched in our Constitution," said Justice Brennan.)[6]

A central aspiration of the tradition has been to achieve justice, and justice has generally been seen to lie partly in the direction marked out by more particular aspirations symbolized by various constitutional provisions regarding human rights. In other words, a central aspiration of the tradition has been to keep faith with the more particular aspirations regarding the form of life of the polity, the life in common. To say this is not to deny that at any given point in the course of the tradition there have been various competing visions of the requirements of justice or that various considerations of self-interest have powerfully distorted the visions and pursuit of justice. Still, a constitutive aspiration of the American political tradition has been to achieve "liberty and justice for all."

If justice can be known and achieved—if, at least, we can make some progress in that direction, as elsewhere I argue we can—is the judicial role that attends my conception of constitutional text and interpretation one way to achieve it?[7] (I am not suggesting it is the only way.) Consider modern constitutional doctrine regarding, for example, freedom of speech, freedom of religion, and racial and other sorts of equality. Imagine what public policy regarding these matters might have been today had the Supreme Court not played a non-originalist role in the modern period. Which body of doctrine—the constitutional doctrine we have or the public doctrine we might well have had—is more defensible as a matter of political morality, as a matter, that is, of the correct interpretation of our tradition, of its aspirations to freedom of expression, freedom of religion, and racial equality? This is not to endorse every detail of modern constitutional doctrine regarding, for example, freedom of speech; it is only to suggest that, on balance, the doctrine we have is sounder than the doctrine we might have had.

"But," you say, "there is no guarantee the Court will not mess up in the future. It has in the past. Remember *Dred Scott* and *Lochner!*" (Or, depending on your point of view, "Look at *Roe v. Wade!*") Certainly the Court is a fallible institution; it has made mistakes and surely will again. In the modern period, however, on balance, the Court's record in the service of individual rights has been admirable. (Even Henry Steele Commager, who in the 1940s criticized the Court's record as irrelevant, if not hostile, to individual rights, has recently sung the Court's praises.) Listen to Robert Cover:

> The 20th century has too often witnessed disastrous and cruel degenerations of majoritarianism into totalitarianism. These calamities have often centered either about state-sponsored persecution of religious, racial or ethnic minorities or party-sponsored manipulation of the machinery of information and politics. The first is an attempt to force "society" into the mold of the "state," the second is the further transformation of the state into the party. These processes can plausibly be understood to be diseases exacerbated by contemporary mass politics which a simple appeal to majorities or supermajorities (Constitutional amendment) is incapable of curing.
>
> It is not clear why the Supreme Court has been capable of exercising leadership and leverage in counteracting such tendencies in the United States for the past 25 or 30 years. But it has done so.[8]

One is not obliged to conclude that, in the modern period, the Court's nonoriginalist role has been an important way (which is not to say the only way) of keeping faith with the tradition's aspiration to justice. I suspect most of us would rather have the burden of defending *that* proposition, however, than the proposition that the Court's role has been ineffective or unimportant.

Why focus on the modern period—the period, roughly, since 1954, when *Brown* v. *Board of Education* was decided? Because the issue for the polity now living is whether any given judicial role is likely to be, "in our own time," as Bickel said, an effective way of keeping faith with the tradition's aspiration to justice. Any answer is, of course, speculative. But what the Court has done in the modern period—in the past generation—seems more indicative of what it is likely to do in our own time, if it continues to play the nonoriginalist judicial role, than what the Court did several generations ago. This is not to deny that what the Court did several generations ago is relevant to our inquiry or to say that what it has done in the past generation is an infallible guide to what it will do in our own time.

Consider now another constitutive aspiration of the American political tradition: the aspiration to electorally accountable government. Is the nonoriginalist role a good way of keeping faith with that aspiration? Because the Court is an electorally unaccountable institution, a larger—that is, nonoriginalist—judicial role is indisputably more problematic than a smaller, originalist one, for the aspiration to electorally accountable government.

My argument, then, is not that the nonoriginalist role the Court has played in the modern period is as good a way as a more constrained role, much less a better way, of keeping faith with the tradition's aspiration to electorally accountable government. The originalist role is a better way of keeping faith with that aspiration. There is, however, that other constitutive aspiration—to justice. My suggestion, which concededly is speculative, but speculation is all we have to go on here, is that what the tradition is likely to gain in justice—that is, in the correct mediation of the past of the tradition with its present—from a judicial role of the nonoriginalist sort the Court has (often) played in the modern period more than offsets what the tradition is likely to lose in "responsiveness" and "accountability."

What is the tradition likely to lose? Certainly the electorate cannot exercise the comparatively direct and immediate political control (through its elected representatives) over the constitutional decisions of the Court that it can exercise over the Court's nonconstitutional decisions. But American history leaves little doubt that when a serious tension develops between the direction in which the Court is leading and the direction in which the electorate, in the end, after deliberation, is determined to move, the electorate, not the Court, will prevail. The various means of political control or influence over the Court—in particular the appointments power and ultimately the amendment power—have proved adequate in that regard.

Constitutional decision making by the Court is responsive to the polity—not immediately, but it is responsive. Still, immediacy counts for something, and there is no denying that time can be lost. (Time is not always lost. In the course of the dialectical interplay between Court and polity I have discussed elsewhere, the political community may eventually come to see it as a good thing that it did not get its way. When that happens, time is not lost. But sometimes time has been lost, as in the case of child labor legislation.) The significance one attaches to that occasional loss depends mainly on the significance one attaches to the actual or potential gain in justice. A black person is more likely to attach greater significance to, to value more highly, the gain, in the modern period, than a white person. Whose point of view is more likely distorted? (In South Africa whose point of view is more likely distorted: the black's or the Afrikaner's?)

Moreover, one who has a strong sense of himself, of his identity, as a participant in a living tradition, whether religious or political, is likely to be more concerned that institutional authority be allocated so that the tradition stands a better chance of getting it right—achieving justice—than that a majority of the community get its way *here and now.*

Does all this seem inconclusive? It *is* inconclusive—*but for originalists no less than for nonoriginalists.* One's decision to accept or reject, one's argument for or against, any conception of judicial role, including the originalist conception, is always *contingent, speculative,* and *provisional* and therefore *revisable.* The decision is contingent because it is rooted partly in one's sense or vision of justice—in one's view of the proper interpretation of the tradition, of the correct mediation of the past of the tradition with its present. The decision is speculative because it is grounded partly on our answers to counterfactual questions about the past and present ("Where would we be today had the Court not played a nonoriginalist role in the past thirty years?") and partly on our predictions of future governmental behavior (both judicial and nonjudicial) on the basis of past behavior. And the decision is provisional and therefore revisable because one's sense or vision of justice may change, one's predictions may prove wrong, or both.

Except for the true believers of various stripes, constitutional theory is, alas, an inconclusive enterprise. How could it be otherwise?

> Designing institutional authority to decide future questions that are, at present, only dimly perceived is inherently uncertain and always revisable in the light of new information. . . . Because all . . . [conceptions of judicial role] . . . are strategic designs, none of them is impervious to constant reassessment and controversy. . . . Because such conceptions are strategic, they are always up for reconsideration. The issue of judicial review can be settled only tentatively, never for all time.[9]

Constitutional Adjudication and Deliberative Politics

Paul Brest has suggested that "the line separating law from politics is not all that distinct and . . . its very location is a question of politics."[10] Certainly the line separating adjudication from politics is "not all that distinct," and its very location—that is, its *proper* location—is a question of politics in the sense of political theory. Indeed, at its (nonoriginalist) best constitutional adjudication is a species of deliberative, transformative politics.

A politics that is merely manipulative and self-serving is one in which citizens and others treat as a given, a fixed point —and thus are un-self-critical toward—what they, individually, want (their preferences) and, therefore, who they, individually, are. (One's commitments, and thus one's wants, are partly self-constitutive.) On this view our political life consists largely of manipulating others—including bargaining with them, to the extent we must—to get what we want. "Fellow humans . . . are not entirely disregarded, but are treated as simply instruments of personal satisfaction: 'Another self is known as the consumer of what I produce, the producer of what I consume, one way or another the assistant in my projects, the servant of my pleasure.' "[11] In manipulative politics there is talk among citizens but not talk in the sense of moral discourse. Participants in manipulative politics "certainly maintain the close identity of politics and talk, but they do so by reducing talk to the dimensions of their smallish politics and turning it into an instrument of symbolic exchange between avaricious but prudent beasts."[12]

It is difficult to imagine a politics that is not manipulative and self-serving to some extent. A deliberative, transformative politics contains an important further dimension, however. Such a politics, in contrast to a politics that is merely manipulative and self-serving, is one in which the questions what ought we to want and, therefore, who ought we to be are open, not closed. Whereas manipulative politics presupposes the authority of existing preferences and is simply an instrument a citizen or group uses to maximize her or its preference satisfaction, deliberative politics is in part an instrument for calling some of our existing preferences into question—for challenging them—and, ultimately, for "the *transformation* of preferences through public and rational discussion."[13] On this view our political life includes continuing moral discourse with one another in an effort to achieve ever more insightful answers to the questions what are our real interests, as opposed to our actual preferences, and thus what sort of persons—with what projects, goals, ideals—ought we to be.

> With regard to fellow humans, the "I-It" contract to desire gives way to an incipient "I-Thou" relationship: "The merely desiring self can go no further than a disingenuous recognition of other selves; in the world *sub specie moris* [as opposed to the world *sub specie voluntatis*], on the other hand, there is a genuine and unqualified recognition of other selves. All other selves are acknowledged to be ends and not merely means to our ends."[14]

Why should we want to cultivate or participate in deliberative politics rather than manipulative politics? What claim does deliberative politics have on us? Any moral community for which love of neighbor *(agape)* is a constitutive ideal—and surely that includes many moral and religious communities in the United States—should understand that ecumenical openness to the Other in discourse facilitates (as well as expresses) such love: I can hardly love the Other—the *real, particular* other—unless I listen to her and, in listening, gain in knowledge of her.

> In genuine human relations, Gadamer notes, the important point is "to experience the Thou truly as a Thou, that means not to ignore his claim and to listen to what he has to say"— an attitude which requires complete existential "openness" and availability. Since openness implies readiness to interrogate and listen to one another, genuine encounter can be said to have the character of a conversation . . . a conversation which, far from being a series of monologues, is governed by the "dialectic of question and answer" and whose distant ancestor is the Platonic dialogue.[15]

Thus we have an other-directed reason for cultivating and participating in deliberative politics.

We also have a self-directed reason: deliberative politics is an essential instrument of self-knowledge. It is a basic premise of deliberative politics that we come to know who we truly are—we come to know our authentic selves, in the sense of what sort of persons we should be and thus what we should want—not monologically, but dialogically. Ronald Beiner's elegant articulation of the premise merits full quotation:

> Human subjects have no privileged access to their own identity and purposes. It is through rational dialogue, and especially through political dialogue, that we clarify, even to ourselves, who we are and what we want. It is mistaken to assume that we necessarily enter into dialogue with an already consolidated view of where we stand and what we are after, conceiving of speech merely as a means to be used for winning over others, rather than as an end to be pursued for its own sake. On the contrary, communication between subjects joined in a community of rational dialogue may entail a process of moral self-discovery that will lead us to a better insight into our own ends and a firmer grasp upon our own subjectivity. Here politics functions as a normative concept, describing what collective agency should be like, rather than abiding by its present devalued meaning. The political expression of this ideal is the republican tradition. Thus inquiry into the intersubjective basis of moral and political rationality may contribute to a fuller understanding of what Arendt and Habermas call a public realm or public space, what Charles Taylor has called a deliberative culture, and what in the traditional vocabulary goes by the name of a republic. Our hope is that such reflection will ultimately

conduct us back to Aristotle's insight that it is through speech and deliberation that man finds the location of his proper humanity, between beast and god, in the life of the citizen.[16]

By now it should be quite clear that moral discourse is a principal constituent of a deliberative, transformative politics.

Given the dissensus that is a prominent feature of a morally pluralistic society like our own—given, that is, what Rawls has referred to as the "subjective circumstances" of justice[17]—how are the political disagreements and conflicts that occasion moral discourse to be resolved? At least, how is progress toward resolution to be achieved? A deliberative, transformative politics and the moral discourse that is one of its principal constituents require political *community*.

> Necessarily, . . . [such questions] must be submitted to criteria of judgment to which (ideally) all those judging can assent. That is, there must be underlying grounds of judgment which human beings, *qua* members of a judging community, share, and which serve to unite in communication even those who disagree *(and who may disagree radically)*. The very act of communication implies some basis of common judgment. There must be some agreement of judgment on what would count as valid historical evidence, or valid moral considerations, such as would tend to confirm or contradict one political judgment or the other (although it may well be that none of these considerations is conclusive). For judgment to be at all possible, there must be standards of judgment, and this implies a community of judgment, that is, agreements in judgment at a deeper level that grounds those at the level of ordinary political argument. In this sense, discourse rests upon an underlying substratum of agreement in judgments. The very possibility of communication means that disagreement and conflict are grounded in a deeper unity. This is what may be termed, borrowing Kantian language, a "transcendental" requirement of our discourse.[18]

One reason some persons are skeptical that a deliberative, transformative politics is available in American society—one reason they think that perhaps only a manipulative, self-serving politics is available—is that they believe that given its morally pluralistic character, American society is not a true community but a city of Babel. In their view the United States is a nation of communities but not itself a community in any significant sense of the term.

In what sense and to what extent is American society a true political community, "a judging community," notwithstanding its morally pluralistic character? It is a true political community in the sense and to the extent that the various moral communities that together constitute the pluralistic society share certain basic aspirations as to how the collective life, the life in common, should be lived. There *are* such shared aspirations: for example, the freedoms of speech, press, and religion, due process of law, and equal protection of the laws. Of course, the aspirations are indeterminate. If they were not indeterminate, they would not be so widely shared: "Our actual shared moral principles . . . have been rendered indeterminate in order to be adequately shared, adequately shared for the purposes of practical life, that is, with persons of quite different and incompatible standpoints."[19] Every large community—including, indeed especially, the American political-constitutional community—comprises dissensus as well as consensus.

To say that the shared aspirations are indeterminate is not to say that they are inconsequential or that the sharing of them is inconsequential. The shared aspirations are what make political judgment possible. They are, for us in the United States, the "underlying grounds of judgment which" we, "*qua* members of a judging community, share, and which serve to unite in communication even those who disagree *(and who may disagree radically)*." Indeed, without such shared (albeit indeterminate) standards of judgment, articulate disagreement would not even be possible. "Even divergent judgments of the most deep-seated and fundamental kind are rooted in some relation of community, otherwise one would lack the concepts with which to disagree."[20] Imagine a disagreement between two persons about a matter concerning, for example, religious liberty. A discursive effort to resolve the disagreement is not likely to get very far, or even begin, if only one of the parties is committed to the ideal of freedom of religion. A discursive effort stands a better chance of making progress if both parties accept the ideal.

Since the principle *is* indeterminate, what work can the ideal (or aspiration, or principle) really do in resolving, or at least diminishing, the disagreement? To accept the ideal of freedom of religion—or any other political-moral ideal—is almost certainly to accept that a particular governmental policy is illegitimate, for example, a policy requiring persons to profess allegiance to religious doctrines to which they conscientiously object. Like other general principles, the principle of freedom of religion is a memorandum of particulars, and in the community that embraces the principle there will be, at any given time, some particulars (at least one)—such as the belief that government may not legitimately compel allegiance to religious doctrines—about which there is a virtual consensus and that therefore constitute the uncontested core of the principle. So parties who accept the principle but disagree about whether policy A violates it can engage in discourse with one another about the respects in which A is relevantly like, or relevantly unlike, another policy or policies that would consensually violate the principle. They can also engage in discourse about the respects in which A is relevantly like or unlike another policy that has been authoritatively held to violate the principle (assuming that the holding is not then in question). Here the role of precedent is apparent. In this way, then, the sharing of principles, even relatively indeterminate ones, serves to ground and focus discursive efforts that otherwise would stand little chance of getting started.

In thus grounding and focusing discursive efforts aimed at diminishing conflict, shared indeterminate principles serve an essential social function: they are an occasion of *the mediation of consensus and dissensus.* In that sense the constitutional text, understood as the symbolization of fundamental aspirations and principles of the American political tradition and community, is a principal occasion of mediating consensus and dissensus.

> The inherently ambiguous character of legal rules [and, we might add, constitutional principles] . . . permits the engagement of parties who submit contending interpretations of legal notions to participate, through the open forum of the court, in the continuous reestablishment of a rule of law that stands as their common property and their warrant of real community. . . . Ambiguous talk makes modern politics possible . . . by tempering the assertion of particular interests and parochial understandings with symbols whose common use, in the face of diverse interpretations, provides a mooring for social solidarity and a continuing invitation to engage in communal discourse. And that continuing invitation, finally, engages us as well in quests for meanings that transcend whatever univocal determinations we have achieved at any given moment.[21]

By this point the sense in which nonoriginalist constitutional adjudication is a species of deliberative, transformative politics (and thus demonstrates that such a politics is available to us notwithstanding the morally pluralistic character of our political community) should be evident. Constitutional discourse is simply political-moral discourse in which the operative basic standards of judgment are the fundamental aspirations of the American political tradition and community symbolized by the Constitution. In constitutional deliberation, as in political deliberation generally, what is at issue . . . is not "what should I do?" or "how should I conduct myself?" but: "how are we to be together, and what is to be the institutional setting for that being-together?" . . . It is not self-deliberation about my life, but mutual deliberation conducted between agents implicated in a common life.[22]

Although in constitutional adjudication the principal "agents" are the parties to constitutional cases (and their lawyers) and the judges, other agents include everyone—public official, editorial writer, public interest lawyer, citizen—who participates in the larger deliberation about the issue or issues in question. At its idealized best, constitutional deliberation among all the "agents implicated in a common life"—and in particular among appellate judges, especially the nine-member Supreme Court—does not proceed in a monologic way, in which judgment is "submitted to one's fellows for confirmation or negation only subsequent to one's having arrived at the judgment independently of them." Rather, constitutional deliberation is dialogical; it proceeds in a way "that does not abstract from one's dicourse with one's fellows." What David Tracy has said recently of conversation holds true of constitutional conversation—that is, of constitutional deliberation as dialogue or discourse:

> Conversation is a game with some hard rules: say only what you mean; say it as accurately as you can; listen to and respect what the other says, however different or other; be willing to correct or defend your opinions if challenged by the conversation partner; be willing to argue if necessary, to confront if demanded, to endure necessary conflict, to change your mind if the evidence suggests it. These are merely some generic rules for questioning. As good rules, they are worth keeping in mind in case the questioning does begin to break down. In a sense they are merely variations of the transcendental imperatives elegantly articulated by Bernard Lonergan: "Be attentive, be intelligent, be responsible, be loving, and, if necessary, change."[23]

Again, moral deliberation requires community. Many persons participate in more than one community (for example, moral, political, intellectual). In the United States everyone is a member not only of some moral or religious community but also of the morally pluralistic political community. Thus a problem arises: When someone engages in moral discourse,

> which community is appealed to for the intersubjective criteria or grounds of judgment, since the latter will vary as one varies the community appealed to. . . . Where allegiances

conflict, it is not decided in advance which community will supply the basis of judgment. Does my commitment to a particular people outweigh, or is it outweighed by, my commitment to some other group?

It [is not] immediately apparent to whom the judgment is addressed: a community of the past or one projected into the future; a particular national community or a community of nations; a tiny circle of associates or universal mankind. . . . Thus, the claim—judgment implies judging community— gives rise to the question: which community?[24]

With respect to the species of political-moral deliberation that is constitutional adjudication, the right answer to the question "which community?" seems clear. Nonoriginalist constitutional adjudication implies and requires the constitutional community—the community comprising those persons and groups in the morally pluralistic society who share a commitment to the aspirations symbolized by the constitutional text. Thus in constitutional-moral discourse the community appealed to for the fundamental "intersubjective criteria or grounds of judgment" is the constitutional community.

Constitutional discourse, then, *at its idealized best,* is the moral discourse of the constitutional community. James Boyd White has argued that

law is most usefully seen not . . . as a system of rules, but as a branch of rhetoric; . . . the kind of rhetoric of which law is a species is most usefully seen not, as law usually is, either as a failed science or the ignoble art of persuasion, but as the central art by which community and culture are established, maintained, and transformed.[25]

As I have presented it, constitutional adjudication is precisely such an enterprise. Nonoriginalist constitutional adjudication is a way—not the only way, but certainly a principal one—in which the constitutional community is established, maintained, and transformed.

Why should we want to establish and maintain the constitutional community? For many—most?—of us, the constitutional community is a splendid achievement, and our membership in it is deeply satisfying, even ennobling. As members of the constitutional community we participate in a form of life that is both a personal and a collective good (good for "me" and good for "us")—a form of life that enables us, both individually and collectively, to make progress, however halting, in realizing our true selves and in achieving well-being. Were we deprived of or cut off—alienated—from the constitutional (or an equivalent) community, in the way the victims of authoritarian and totalitarian societies are deprived of such a community, we would, we believe, be seriously diminished. (Membership in the constitutional community need not compete with or detract from membership in other communities, some doubtless more important to us than the constitutional community, including some communities more local than the constitutional community, such as family, and some more universal, such as church.) Why should we want to transform the constitutional community? Because, like any human community, the constitutional community is inevitably and always imperfect and therefore inevitably and always in need of revision.

I want to return to the question of the relation between constitutional adjudication and deliberative politics. Constitutional adjudication has a discursive character that is external as well as internal. It is internal in that the discourse is among the principal constitutional decision makers, the judges themselves, especially the justices of the Supreme Court. It is external in that the discourse is between the judiciary, especially the Court, and the political community as a whole. Because of its internal discursive character, constitutional adjudication (at its idealized best) is itself a species of deliberative, transformative politics—in which the judges serve as representatives of the political community. As Justice Brennan has said: "When Justices [of the Supreme Court] interpret the Constitution they speak for their community, not for themselves alone. The act of interpretation must be undertaken with full consciousness that it is, in a very real sense, the community's interpretation that is sought."[26]

Because of its external discursive character, constitutional adjudication is an aspect of a larger deliberative, transformative politics—in which the judges serve as interlocutors of the political community and its elected representatives. Indeed, to the extent that constitutional adjudication is disturbing and even prophetic, it can serve to precipitate in the political community, or enhance, a careful deliberation of certain issues as "matters of principle." This is a crucial function in a society in which a variety of constraints—for example, the value legislators place on incumbency, the sheer volume and complexity of the issues with which legislators must try to find time to deal, and a skepticism about the possibility of productive moral discourse—inhibit careful deliberation about matters of principle.

Some persons are skeptical about the possibility of a deliberative, transformative politics. Others who are not skeptical think that such a politics is for citizens and their political representatives but not for the courts. My position, as I hope I have made clear, is that such a politics is not only for citizens and their representatives but for the courts as well—and that indeed the courts have an important role to play in encouraging citizens and their representatives to take seriously the possibility of a deliberative politics. The courts play that role by (1) exemplifying such a politics in their discursive practice and (2) engaging the other branches and agencies of government in the sort of discourse that is a prime constituent of deliberative, transformative politics.

Consider the matter from a somewhat different perspective: The constitutional aspirations of the American political community constitute a conception of the good for that community—a conception of how the community should live its collective life, its life in common, if it is to flourish as a political community. The nonoriginalist judicial role I have elaborated here is one way of helping the community to attend to—to remain faithful to—its constitutional conception of the common good. In other words, the nonoriginalist judicial role—more generally, deliberative, transformative politics, of which the nonoriginalist role is a species—is a way of institutionalizing the ideal of self-critical rationality, which is an ideal, an aspiration, of the community. My nonoriginalist constitutional theory is an elaboration of the view that, as I said, the courts, too, have an important role to play.

Notes

1. The longer work from which these reflections are drawn is titled *Morality, Politics, and Law: A Bicentennial Essay.* It was published by the Oxford University Press in 1988.

2. Robert McCloskey, *The American Supreme Court* (Chicago: University of Chicago Press, 1960), pp. 12–13. Cf. Alexander Bickel, *The Least Dangerous Branch* (Indianapolis, Ind.: Bobbs-Merrill, 1962), pp. 27–28: "Democratic government under law—the slogan pulls in two opposed directions, but that does not keep it from being applicable to an operative polity. If it carries the elements of explosion, it doesn't contain a critical mass of them. Yet, if the critical mass is not to be reached, there must be an accommodation, a degree of concord between the diverging elements."

3. Michael Perry, *The Constitution, the Courts, and Human Rights* (New Haven, Conn.: Yale University Press, 1982).

4. Jack Rakove, "Original Meanings of the Constitution: The Historian's Contribution" (Unpublished ms., 1985), pp. 22, 23. See Benjamin Barber, *Strong Democracy: Participatory Politics for a New Age* (Berkeley: University of California Press, 1984), p. 17: "In reality the American political system places many curbs on majoritarianism, and it is probably correct to say with Louis Hartz that 'what must be accounted one of the tamest, mildest, and most unimaginative majorities in modern political history has been bound down by a set of restrictions that betray fanatical terror.' "

5. Larry Alexander, "Painting without Numbers: Noninterpretive Judicial Review," *University of Dayton Law Review,* vol. 8 (1983), pp. 447, 458.

6. William J. Brennan, "The Constitution of the United States: Contemporary Ratification," *South Texas Law Review,* vol. 27 (1986), p. 433.

7. Perry, *Morality, Politics, and Law,* chap. 2.

8. Robert Cover, Book Review, *New Republic,* January 14, 1978, pp. 26, 28.

9. Alexander, "Painting without Numbers," pp. 462–63.

10. Paul Brest, "Interpretation and Interest," *Stanford Law Review,* vol. 34 (1982), pp. 765, 773.

11. Fred Dallmayr, *Polis and Praxis: Exercises in Contemporary Political Theory* (Cambridge, Mass.: MIT Press, 1984), p. 211, quoting Oakeshott, "The Voice of Poetry in the Conversation of Mankind," in Michael Oakeshott, *Rationalism and Politics* (New York: Basic Books, 1962), pp. 206–10.

12. Barber, *Strong Democracy,* pp. 173–74.

13. Joan Elster, "Sour Grapes—Utilitarianism and the Genesis of Wants," in Amartya Sen and Bernard Williams, *Utilitarianism and Beyond* (Cambridge: University of Cambridge Press, 1981), pp. 219, 237.

14. Dallmayr, *Polis and Praxis,* p. 211, quoting Oakeshott, "The Voice of Poetry."

The distinction between deliberative politics and manipulative politics is largely the same as Cass Sunstein's distinction between the "republican" and the "pluralist" conceptions of politics. Sunstein's elaboration of the distinction is illuminating. See Sunstein, "Interest Groups in American Public Law," *Stanford Law Review,* vol. 38 (1985), pp. 29, 31–35.

15. Dallmayr, *Polis and Praxis,* p. 196, quoting Hans-Georg Gadamer, *Truth and Method* (New York: Crossroad, 1900), pp. 321, 323–25.

16. Ronald Beiner, *Political Judgment* (Chicago: University of Chicago Press, 1984), p. 152. See Singer, "The Player and the Cards: Nihilism and Legal Theory," *Yale Law Journal,* vol. 94 (1984), pp. 1, 64–65.

17. See Perry, *Morality, Politics, and Law,* chap. 3.

18. Beiner, *Political Judgment,* pp. 142–43; see also pp. 129–52; and Alasdair MacIntyre, "Moral Arguments and Social Contexts," *Journal of Philosophy,* vol. 80 (1983), p. 590.

19. Alasdair MacIntyre, "Does Applied Ethics Rest on a Mistake?" *Monist,* vol. 67 (1984), pp. 498, 510. See Herbert McCloskey and Alida Brill, *Dimensions of Tolerance: What Americans Believe about Civil Liberties* (New York: Russell Sage Foundation, 1983), pp. 48–58; Prothro and Grigg, "Fundamental Principles of Democracy: Bases of Agreement and Disagreement," *Journal of Politics,* vol. 22 (1960), p. 276. My thanks to Erwin Chemerinsky for the McCloskey/Brill and Prothro/Grigg citations.

20. Beiner, *Political Judgment,* p. 141; cf. pp. 138–44.

21. David Levine, *The Flight from Ambiguity* (Chicago: University of Chicago Press, 1985), pp. 42–43; see also pp. 41–43.

22. Beiner, *Political Judgment,* pp. 138–39.

23. David Tracy, *Plurality and Ambiguity* (San Francisco: Harper and Row, 1987), p. 19, quoting Bernard Lonergan, *Method in Theology* (New York: Herder and Herder, 1972), p. 231; see p. 26 and pp. 26–27: "Arguments on ideal-speech conditions are transcendental in the sense that they claim to provide the necessary conditions for a contingent situation, namely, the implicit claim

to validity in all communication. This is a claim to contingent, not absolute necessity. By contrast, transcendental arguments on the existence or nonexistence of the universe or God are strictly transcendental arguments. Communication could be other than it is, but in fact is not. We reason discursively. We inquire. We converse. We argue. We are human beings, not angels."

24. Beiner, *Political Judgment*, pp. 142–43, 146 (passages rearranged).

25. James B. White, "Law as Rhetoric, Rhetoric as Law: The Arts of Cultural and Communal Life," *University of Chicago Law Review*, vol. 52 (1985), p. 684.

26. Brennan, "Constitution of the United States."

6
Difficulties of Equal Dignity:
The Court and the Family

Robert K. Faulkner

Is it fair to treat all persons as if they are equal in human dignity?

The question seems oddly abstract, if not morally impertinent. It is nevertheless an important question, perhaps the most important question to ask about the post–New Deal Supreme Court's application of the Constitution. The "sparkling vision of the human dignity of every individual," as Justice William Brennan calls the spirit of many recent constitutional initiatives, has a darker side.[1] It is a side not confronted by the Court's friends and not directly confronted, for that matter, by many of its critics.

The cause of human dignity seems impervious to serious question because it seems the cause of humanity, a cause unlimited by partial and parochial divisions. Its adherents disdain the earlier advocates of equal rights, such as Thomas Jefferson and Abraham Lincoln. The older liberal democrats supposed that a portion of a person's dignity depended upon effort and accomplishment and that one might forfeit much or all of human dignity by evil or monstrous conduct. But such an outlook, it is now said, was shaded by individualistic prejudices that have been made obsolete by the development of society. The rights of life, liberty, and opportunity seem merely elitist and selfish in light of an interdependent and hierarchical economy and a more liberating and humane idealism. Fundamentally, a moral progress makes us now aware of society's repression through history of whole classes of persons. We now understand the primacy of world society and the morality of liberating persons from the stereotypes and repressions of the past. This idealistic activism defines us as moral and rational, as opposed to ethnocentric and self-interested. Activists know, for example, that sexism and racism, not lewdness and immodesty, are the real obscenities. To be human is to be an idealistic visionary or a movement activist, and a humane judge should decide disputes and shape law accordingly. The only right

93

question, it follows, is a "how-to" question. To doubt the principle of equal human dignity seems elitist or bigoted. It presumes that some classes of people are superior to others.

Despite its sweeping appeal, thoughtful adherents have been unable to rest in practice with so simple a moralism. Unless one is content to be an ideologue or an extremist, even how-to questions require one to weigh the comparative merit of equal dignity. How should schools, for example, rank the relative priority of equal respect for students, compared with the benefit of assignment to remedial or accelerated classes? While one can minimize the indignities, perhaps, by substituting "exceptional" or "special" for both "remedial" and "accelerated," the superiorities and inferiorities are hardly less for the semantic evasion of candor. To know how far to press an insistence on equal respect, one must ask how beneficial it is in light of other things to be respected, such as free speech or good education, and of bad things, such as incompetence or boredom. If one values candor, one must also admit that respect for individuals should differ to some extent with their qualities or fitness, for example, with the extent that they are truthful, well educated, competent for the job at hand, and interesting. Is not the vision of equal dignity perhaps an astigmatism, a preoccupation with equality that prevents acknowledgment of the various human qualities and of the different respect owed to those who possess them in different degrees?

Nor can a supposition of historical progress relieve one from thinking out the meaning, limits, and defects of the principle one deems superior. Being superior is not the same as being perfect. A flawed vision, moreover, may misread progress. Has the principle of equal dignity evolved with the historical development of mind, or is it merely "moral theory," as its leading proponent in the law schools, Laurence Tribe, calls it at times? It is what Tribe would not acknowledge: a now-fashionable theory propagated by professors in law schools and universities who chance to be influenced by the philosophical odd couple—a democratized neo-Kantian account of moral dignity, itself now infiltrated by Nietzschean theories of antimoral liberation.

While many critics of the contemporary court blame professors, lawyers, and judges, they acknowledge good will and concentrate on exposing bad consequences. It is said that modern liberal judges may have worthy aims, such as perfect justice in trials or integration of the races so that they recognize one another as equals, but such judges misfire in their policy analysis. Elaborate procedural safeguards often impede punishment of precisely those criminals who prey on the vulnerable; busing to integrate often causes disintegration of schools, neighborhoods, and whole cities. In a fit of zealous moralism a "rights industry" has ended up "disabling" churches, schools, and even law and order.[2]

These criticisms touch a very large and vulnerable Achilles' heel. Contemporary legal moralism, committed to a vision of equal and autonomous individuals, slights variety, particular and sectional strengths, and institutional and social needs and arrangements. It suspects these, and all pragmatic balancing, to be excuses for exploitative hierarchy and the status quo. While the critics confront the heel, however, they often shy from the head. Let justice be done, the idealist will say, whatever the inconvenience or cost.

It is, for example, worse to convict innocents than to let the guilty go free, Justice Brennan says, for punishment strips a man of his dignity. If the maxim might be traditional in orthodox Anglo-Saxon legal doctrine, the reason is not. In general, "There is no better test of a society than how it treats those accused of transgressing against it."[3] This seems a test of a society's capacity for self-destruction. Does not Justice Brennan's measure put solicitude for lawbreakers and enemies ahead of solicitude for the law-abiding, the contributors, and the patriots? Justice Brennan seems to suppose that sticking up for the country and its citizens reflects only the interests of the system and its beneficiaries. Suppose, however, the system is broadly a good one and its beneficiaries include a broad majority. Justice Brennan's attack turns out to be unrelenting and undiscriminating. He attacks any "political orthodoxy from above,"[4] not least that of the patriotic and law-abiding.

This radicalizes the difficulty. Primacy is given to those who challenge not only the country's laws but also, and especially, the country's whole government and its principles of government, society, and rights. Whatever Justice Brennan's intentions, his doctrine suggests that the test of even a just society is its capacity for disabling what it upholds as just and advantageous. His suspicion, after all, is directed at any political orthodoxy from above. A generalized suspicion of the establishment, without respect to the degree of its justice, and a generalized liberation of those hitherto looked down upon, whether justly or not, replace an equitable judgment of cases and of deserts.

There is a paradox here, one not innocuous but dangerous. Justice Brennan's insistent preaching against political orthodoxy amounts to a dominating orthodoxy and a corrosively impolitic orthodoxy at that. The new creed undermines liberal democracy by radicalizing certain of its principles: equality of rights or needs is replaced by "egalitarianism"; liberal rights are replaced by "libertarian" freedom.[5] It is true that judges defend the new creed as nonpolitical, as a vision untainted by interests and majorities. The claim of purity, however, only exacerbates the doctrinairism: the vision is inherently controversial, politically as well as morally. Amounting to a provocative counterculture, it is at war with traditional creeds and morals, especially religious faith and sexual morals. A revolutionary attack on middle-class culture justifies a peculiarly antimoral and antireligious domination by judges, administrators, and committees of academics and activists, some of the least democratic instruments of a modern society.

How just, then, is the vision of equal dignity? It harbors a difficulty in principle, apart from impracticality and extremism in application. Dignity is to some extent like honor: if everyone has it equally, no one has it. If all persons are entitled to respect, whether their behavior or character is respected, such respect does not amount to much. Granted, dignity is not simply like honor. All human beings are owed a basic consideration; basic rights to life, liberty, and self-advancement are to be respected. Basic respect, however, is not equal respect. If equal respect for persons fails to respect important differences, it must be hollow and hypocritical or else blind to distinctions of desert.

In practice, many generous people devoted to the cause of equal dignity modify their creed with judgments about relative merit and decency. These compromises nevertheless fly in the teeth of an incompatible doctrine. The results typically slight the deserving and exact undeserved respect for the vulgar, the vicious, and the criminal. To that extent the doctrine of equal respect promotes injustice.

One will never understand the power of this creed, however, unless one confronts its great claim: at least the principle of equal dignity precludes discrimination on arbitrary grounds such as race, color, or ethnic origin. There is truth in this. People deserve to be judged according to real merits: not "by the color of their skin but by the content of their character," as Martin Luther King, Jr., characteristically put it.[6] It is also true, though, that they deserve to have their real merits, "the contents of their character," judged and respected. These ought not be denied, whether by traditional prejudices or by a new prejudice that respect for all is the only important principle. I acknowledge easily, I would even insist, that unequal respect is too often given according to irrelevant differences in race, wealth, popularity, celebrity, or power. The remedy is wise judgment about genuine worth, however, not a systematically indiscriminate denial of differences in worth. Otherwise, one fails to do justice even to those who contribute most to the humane cause of civil rights. It would be obviously unfair to attribute to a King or to an Abraham Lincoln only the dignity or moral stature of everyman.

These considerations show that the ideal of equal dignity is questionable on its face. They do not show the new spirit as the Supreme Court has applied it, perhaps in better formulations or with wise compromises.

Judicial Formulations

Recent Supreme Courts have extended in an unprecedented manner the scope of the Fourteenth Amendment's command: "no state" shall "deny to any person within its jurisdiction the equal protection of the laws." The Court's suspicion of racial or even ethnic discriminations might be thought to follow the amendment's special concern, just after the Civil War, for the newly freed blacks. Its rescuing of aliens from partial laws may be traced back to 1886, when a Chinese laundry operator was protected in his "right of an occupation."[7] But the Courts of the past fifty years were the first to extend "suspected classifications" to laws discriminating, say, between male and female on pay or ability to act as parent; illegitimate and legitimate children with respect to a right to inherit; married and unmarried on the availability of contraceptives; residents and nonresidents on eligibility for welfare; and voters of more or less voting power with respect to apportionment by district. A new purpose showed itself. The Court did not limit itself to the old civil rights to engage in a trade or occupation; to sue, to receive the protection of law and police; and to serve on juries and in public office. It defended rights of a new sort: to be free of the stigma of inferiority that causes psychological suffering, to travel or migrate, and to have "privacy," "self-expression," and satisfaction of "basic needs." One can speak of entitlements, rights not merely to the opportunities of civil society but to be treated as if possessing equal dignity and to be provided one's basic sustenance.

A new priority was given this policy. While the Fourteenth Amendment prohibits only "state" actions, the Court has expanded the concept of state action and thus narrowed the sphere of private actions exempted from judicial supervision. If often requires that the "state interest" be "compelling" in order to justify laws or regulations impinging on the rights it upholds. The new principle of equal dignity has thus led the U.S. Supreme Court to a new public dignity and power: enforcing novel policies by extending a pervasive pressure for equal dignity to schools, electoral districts, prisons, sexual relations, and a host of other areas.

For a closer examination, I turn to recent cases involving sexual or familial matters, in which claims to equal dignity and personal autonomy confront an elemental passion and the elemental association. In

97

its new spirit of liberation the contemporary Court tends in certain crucial cases to interpret married couples as but couples and couples as but voluntary associations of autonomous individuals, and to understand individuals as possessed of a right of privacy not to be much limited by considerations of morality. There is a tendency to define the private and hence the most intimate as fundamental and even to suppose that by free sexual choice the individual autonomously defines himself or herself, or perhaps itself. Social standards such as legitimacy of birth and natural standards such as gender come to be suspect as repressive stereotypes.

Children, Abortion, and Sex as Private Rights

Consider a little commentary on the authority to have and raise a child, from *Eisenstadt* v. *Baird* (1972).[8] *Eisenstadt* struck down a Massachusetts law that prohibited distribution of contraceptives to single persons except by physician or pharmacist. The statute was passed subsequent to an earlier Supreme Court decision, in *Griswold* v. *Connecticut* (1965), which had prohibited bans on selling contraceptives to married couples.[9] My point regards not the holding, for the sale of contraceptives might be defended (or limited) on a variety of public and private grounds, but rather the special ground, a "right of privacy" that trumps the legislature's distinction between married and unmarried. "It is true that in *Griswold* the right of privacy in question inhered in the marital relationship," wrote Justice Brennan:

> Yet the marital couple is not an independent entity with a mind and heart of its own, but an association of two individuals each with a separate intellectual and emotional makeup. If the right of privacy means anything, it is the right of the *individual*, single or married, to be free from unwarranted governmental intrusion into matters so fundamentally affecting a person as the decision whether to bear or beget a child.

So understood, the right of privacy makes bearing or begetting a child the responsibility of the individual, or perhaps a couple of individuals, not the family in the sense of a married couple. Justice Brennan acknowledges that the state might have wished to discourage quack remedies or premarital sex or had other concerns about health or morals. Yet he finesses these considerations without confronting them. He does not take them seriously.

Justice Brennan also abstracts from a related matter of social policy: the importance to children of families that care, inspire, and discipline. Is any individual, or any pairing of individuals, likely to be the sort of family to provide a good upbringing? The question can be rhetorical, because the answer is obvious in the United States: the burgeoning of one-parent families, of failure by fathers to bear the costs or duties of upbringing, of births out of wedlock, and of hardships for the children involved with indifferent parents, hardly any parents, divorced parents, the single parent. More than 40 percent of births among white teenage girls were out of wedlock in 1984; the figure was 89.5 percent among black teenage girls. In fewer than twenty-five years, out-of-wedlock teen births for all races rose from 15.4 percent in 1960 to 56.3 percent in 1984. Should one be cavalier in encouraging any person, or two persons, in their "choice" to have a child? Those devoted to the poor should be most troubled. The deterioration in family life especially affects poor children whose other associations are too often bleak and debilitating, and it contributes to their poverty. As a rule, according to two authorities on the subject, "An out-of-wedlock birth to a young mother is a direct path to long-term poverty and welfare dependency."[10] While these considerations may suggest a social policy favoring contraception or abortion, the Court's policy is "pro-choice," rather than for wise choice, be it public or private.

The most famous judicial establishment of the right of choice is to a woman's choice about abortion. Compared with any other country, indeed, the distinction of American abortion law is the extent of abortion on demand, in particular the mother's demand. That is the conclusion of Mary Ann Glendon, who recently compared the abortion policies of twenty Western nations.[11] While there was for some time a general easing of the legal requirements for abortion, she concludes, only five countries (Austria, Denmark, Greece, Norway, and Sweden), besides the United States, have legalized abortion on demand. Among these, only the United States forbids *any* state regulation of abortion to preserve the fetus until viability (the twenty-fourth to twenty-eighth week, according to the Supreme Court in 1973), fails to require regulation to protect the fetus after viability, forgoes and discourages waiting periods and consultations for due consideration by the woman and her family, and is governed by courts that "shut down the legislative process of bargaining, education, and persuasion on the abortion issue."[12] The United States is unusual among the six countries in providing neither adequate public support for mothers nor especially efficient enforcement of child support from absent parents.[13] Nowhere in the developed world, but only in China, with its vast and ruthless population control policy, did Glendon find "a country where the legal approach to abortion is as indifferent to unborn life as it is in the United States."[14] She traced the "American difference" to a bare right of autonomous individuals to privacy.

Let us ask a question Glendon only intimates in her book. Is the right of privacy merely a right to private indulgence? Does it dull one to regard for others, the born as well as the unborn? If so, if it is simply a claim to private satisfactions, it lacks a concern for justice in the obvious sense. Yet the principle suggests more. It at once encourages individuals to do as they wish and subjects their wishes to principle. Principled liberation differs from ordinary freedom wished by ordinary people: on principle one must allow others to be unprincipled. One should be "nonjudgmental," to use the current vernacular. Moral relativism is constitutionally established. One can indulge oneself so long as one does not indulge one's moral opinions. To be nonjudgmental is to obey scrupulously the judgment that one should wash the brain of scruples over what is good and bad. In this sense, liberation is antimoral brainwashing.

In elaborating the right of privacy in *Eisenstadt*, Justice Brennan relied on the authority of *Stanley v. Georgia*.[15] *Stanley* held that the First Amendment, when prohibiting laws abridging freedom of speech or press, implies the right in one's home to have and watch pornographic movies. The reasoning, by Justice Thurgood Marshall, exhibits in microcosm the judges' reformulation of the First Amendment into a warrant for a peculiarly private self-expression. This is often called an evolution. It seems a devolution. Justice Marshall deprecates the public or interpersonal connotations of "speech" and "press" by equating them with a private right "to receive ideas and information." He expressly excludes any qualification of "social worth," in accord with past cases, and reorients liberty in accord with a "fundamental" suspicion of governmental intrusions into "privacy." Then he extends Justice Louis Brandeis's defense of privacy, for the exercise of "man's spiritual nature, of his feelings and of his intellect," to the viewing of pornographic movies.

Let us suppose that such trifling voyeurism, out of the public eye, should often be tolerated by the laws of a free, big, heterogeneous, and tolerant country. Must the spirit of the law move from tolerance to equal respect and thus grant respectability and the law's patronage and encouragement? What were once called blue movies or stag movies are now commonly called adult movies. Justice Marshall's reply is: "The line between the transmission of ideas and mere entertainment is much too elusive for this Court to draw, if indeed such a line can be drawn at all."[16]

Is it so difficult to tell an idea from the pleasure of an orgasm? Indeed, does Justice Marshall think it possible not to tell them apart? Even if that distinction were blurred, there is an obvious difference between ideas regarding important public matters, as in the Court's opinions, and ideas that appeal to sensations and the sensational, as in the typical scandal sheet or hard-core magazine. It seems banal to recount the obvious—but it is worse to forget it. Justice Marshall is so eager to free self-expression from disdain or limit that he disdains moral distinctions, even obvious distinctions of the quality of entertainment and enlightenment. To miss the distinction, however, is to miss the thing. He equates a porno flick with entertainment, without differentiating entertainment from low entertainment, and then equates it with "the transmission of ideas." Recall Jefferson's wish for a citizenry enlightened by newspapers and education. Then consider this extension of the constitutional right of speech and press to a voyeur's cheap thrills from a movie in the dark. If this be dignity, let us have our degradation straight, without the varnish of judicial hypocrisy.

Georgia had asserted "the right to protect the individual's mind from the effects of obscenity," if only for the sake of public morality. In reply Justice Marshall quoted another Court decision on obscenity: "The Constitutional guarantee is not confined to the expression of ideas that are conventional or shared by a majority." A state's solicitude for the quality of public life is reduced to mere artificial custom, perhaps only the imposition of a majority. Morality is but artifice, and imposition may be disdained by true partisans of rights.

Not surprisingly, a right of privacy comes to be focused on things most intimate, on the private parts. Justice Harry A. Blackmun wrote recently in dissent: "The right of an individual to conduct intimate relationships in the intimacy of his or her own home seems to be the heart of the Constitution's protection of privacy."[17] While the right of privacy encourages sex according to principle and as part of a political movement, its principle is autonomy, the politics of liberation from restraints. It encourages a peculiarly self-regarding sexual activity, a private titillation removed from both responsibility and the higher charms and delights of erotic love and interesting marriages. The outlook seems somewhat more male than female, looking more to quick pleasure and promiscuity, less to scruple and commitment. Its popularization tends, no doubt, to undermine modesty and decent tastes. It must erode the severe spirit that contributes to public service and devotion to duty. It must provoke, it has provoked, a variety of indignant moral and moralistic reactions.

The Court has drawn back somewhat from the moral nihilism prescribed by *Stanley*. In two opinions by Chief Justice Warren Burger, a slim majority interpreted the First Amendment in particular to provide principally for speech, especially for political discussion. Protection of doubtful material was reserved for works of "serious literary value." In regulating obscenity, Chief Justice Burger said, a state might give priority to "public safety" and the "public morality," to "decent society," "quality of life and total community environment," the "tone of commerce in great city centers," and "the social interest in order and morality."[18] Such doctrines have spread a bit. The Court has upheld anti–skid row zoning laws that concentrated or spread out the locations of porno theaters. There is, Justice John Paul Stevens wrote in the leading case, "a less vital interest in the uninhibited exhibition of material that is on the borderline between pornography and artistic expression, than in the free dissemination of ideas of social and political significance." A city may provide for "the character of its neighborhoods" and for "stable neighborhoods," against an "urban jungle" and the "blighting" of surrounding areas.[19] A minority of four denounced the majority's decision as an "aberration," that contained an "alien concept" of discrimination among kinds of expression. Yet *American Mini-Theaters* permitted a community to regulate only location of pornographic theaters, not, say, to ban them from city limits. The implications of *Miller* and *Paris Adult Theater* for First Amendment law have not spread much beyond a narrowly circumscribed struggle over hard-core pornography.

In *Bowers* v. *Harwick* the Court recently delivered a deeper challenge to Justice Marshall's gloss on the right of privacy.[20] *Bowers* held that homosexual sodomy is not constitutionally protected by a right of privacy under the First or Fourteenth Amendments and in general that there is not a constitutional right to sexual expression. An opinion for the Court by Justice Byron White managed to distinguish *Griswold*, *Eisenstadt*, and *Roe* as cases involving a right whether to beget a child, as if they chiefly approved privacy in the context of family, marriage, and procreation. *Stanley* was distinguished as dealing with the First Amendment. The cases, Justice White contended, do not stand "for the proposition that any kind of private sex conduct between consenting adults is constitutionally insulated from state proscription"; nor is such a protection "implicit in the important measures of liberty: the concept of ordered liberty or the deep roots of the nation's history or traditions."

Four justices dissented. In an opinion joined by Justices Brennan and Marshall, Justice Blackmun accused the majority of ignoring "the values that underlie the Constitutional right of privacy." He was right.

Justice White had evinced impatience with judicial invention of "new rights" and had danced around the right of privacy in particular. Justice Blackmun expounded what Justice White deprecated. He attacked the majority's reliance on the country's traditions and moral beliefs and the supposition that the rights in question might be measured against the "general public welfare." The rights of privacy are prior because "they form so central a part of an individual's life." More precisely, they allow the individual to define his or her own form: "to define one's identity." The most intimate sexual choices alter "so dramatically an individual's own self-definition."

Here is abstract theory with a vengeance and with all the murkiness of some up-to-the-minute philosophizing. Consider the supposition that each of us is to make himself or herself or itself. If the individual is self-defined, is there any self prior to the definition? If so, the self is not simply self-defining. If not, there is nothing to do the defining. This version of individualism is murky all the way to a core so hollow as to be nothing: the aimless hollow self.

Such a doctrine abstracts airily from the obvious. Is sexual intimacy chiefly about self-definition? Or is it, in different circumstances and manifestations, about desire, lust, beauty, domination, love, brutality, pleasure, passion, delight, children, secret affairs, family—a panoply of important experiences and consequences whose proper definition and regulation are at times grossly obvious and at times subtly complicated? How to regard necrophilia is easy to decide; births out of wedlock, more difficult; homosexuality, more complicated yet. Grant that how one loves affects what one is. So does one's unchosen sex, one's chosen occupation, one's unchosen and chosen family, one's unchosen and chosen schooling, one's role models, the character of neighborhood and customs, and the celebrities and leaders one looks up to. The strange doctrine of the primacy of the right to sexual choice abstracts from the many other important influences needed for a good character and a good life. As Justice Blackmun would apply that doctrine in *Bowers*, it dominates and erodes those influences, and for the sake of an empty and self-denying self.

Bowers arose when Georgia police entered Hardwick's residence with a search warrant and chanced to discover him in a homosexual act. In fact the Georgia law outlawing sodomy (heterosexual as well as homosexual) had rarely been enforced in recent years, and Georgia officials declined to press charges in this case. It was Hardwick who took the occasion to challenge the law and, in effect, Georgia's not unusual dialectic between an announced profamily policy, as one might call it, and an unannounced tolerance for some other sexual practices. In response to the exposure of its subtle mixture of rule and

103

equity and to the challenge to its law, Georgia contended for the "right of the Nation and of the States to maintain a decent society." In dissent Justice Blackmun set forth the principle that fells all established principles: the test of the protection of free expression "is the right to differ as to things that touch the heart of the existing order."

Legitimacy and Sex as Repressive Stereotypes

Not surprisingly, the new judicial doctrines of individuality are best defended by Justice Brennan, notably in his revealing attacks upon laws that classify by legitimacy of birth and by sex. Not surprisingly, also, the underpinnings are theoretical and touched with zeal. Beneath the new doctrine of the equality of persons is a general critique of repressive society and a glowing animus that belies the justice's public talk of the country's original sparkling vision.

The Supreme Court now routinely strikes down state regulations that favor legitimate children over "nonmarital children," a sharp turn from *Labine* v. *Vincent* (1971).[21] In *Labine* a majority of justices had held that Louisiana might give priority to legitimates in sharing property left without a will. Justice Hugo Black tersely acknowledged the state's purposes: encouragement of family life and regulation of property. Justice John Marshall Harlan added that a state might reasonably impose on a married man "obligations to any resulting offspring beyond those which he owes to the products of a casual liaison." The arguments distinguish marriage as a more serious and legally regulated relationship that a state might wisely prefer and encourage. Nevertheless, a dissent by Justice Brennan is the powerful opinion—in emotion, comprehensive argument, number of pages, and eventual influence. Its spirit moved later majorities, notably behind White in *Stanley* v. *Illinois* and Powell in *Weber* v. *Aetna*.[22] Pity the suffering illegitimates—and down with laws embodying the "moral prejudice of bygone centuries which vindictively punished not the illegimate's parents, but also the hapless, and innocent children." Moral indignation suffuses Justice Brennan's remarks, but it is aimed at "moral prejudice," the still common disdain for illegitimacy. There is a virtue in his outlook: why should children suffer for the "misdeeds of their parents?" Yet there is also a defect. This prejudice is only the other side of a decent opinion that holds sexual relations in marriage right and birth in marriage right, and those children born out of wedlock, often from casual liaisons, not quite right. In effect, Justice Brennan exaggerates the old outlook by equating its judgments with punishments and dismisses its reasonable side as but prejudice. He need not consider how to balance both the welfare of the child and the encouragement of childbearing within marriage. Instead Justice Brennan proclaims the antimoral razor: the supposition of a liberating advance beyond the morality that oppressed "bygone centuries." There is an indignant suspicion of all restraints not self-imposed. And there is a complacent belief in progress that allows indignation to flourish; Justice Brennan supposes that a new liberation is without risk of a new degradation or anarchy. He need not be solicitous of marital duty as well as individual liberty, of moral and social restraints as well as self-expression. History will provide.

This historico-cultural advocacy of liberation from morality originated largely in the dangerous reflections of Friedrich Nietzsche. All morality now, Nietzsche had argued, is fundamentally repression by a timid middle class of authentic creativity by the strong. Nietzsche meant his critique, however, to destroy the modern democracy he despised. Justice Brennan inadvertently introduces the anti-democratic enemy into the constitutional citadel. He enforces Nietzsche's attack upon moral "values" in a version democratized to justify equal respect. Why, however, should liberation and progress deprive liberal democrats of the benefits of a propitious upbringing and a promising character?

The *Labine* dissent provides an answer that is a revealing evasion. There is no relevant difference between children legitimate and illegitimate, Justice Brennan argues, since "biologically" they are similar in origin, and "spiritually" they are part of a "warm, familial relationship." The first is indisputable. The second is fatuous. Justice Brennan seems to suppose all relations of child-begetting to be families (which was always false and gains no truth in the liberated decades), and all families equal. He treats marriage as but "formalities," useful chiefly in aiding the state to distribute property efficiently. Filtered through the equal dignity of persons, marriage, like the family, dissolves in a solvent of self-expressing individualism and indiscriminate compassion.

The underlying rationale appears in a powerful opinion by Justice Brennan that finally won a Supreme Court majority for a "women's liberation" outlook. Sex-based classifications are suspect, he writes for the Court in *Frontiero v. Richardson*.[23] We are given the familiar historico-cultural explanation: such distinctions reflect the "long and unfortunate history of sex discrimination" in America. The United States has been an oppressor nation, which has kept women "not on a pedestal, but in a cage." Justice Brennan expressly treats as benighted sexists Alexis de Tocqueville, who celebrated American democracy as a model for the world and women as its moral educators, and Thomas Jefferson, who refounded the country more democratically. The old attitudes violate "the basic concept" of our legal system, that legal burdens bear some relation to individual responsibility "or to ability to perform or contribute to society."

Let us agree for now that this is our basic legal concept. Do reasonable sex-based classifications in fact violate it? Might one reasonably favor special policies that encourage women to "perform or contribute" in home and family? Justice Brennan's principle does not justify his conclusion. Still, the Court has followed his conclusion. It has overthrown laws that require spouses of female military officers to prove receipt of over one-half support before being classified as a dependent, that would grant custody of a child to its unmarried mother rather than its father, or that prefer a man before a woman as executor. While the Court has occasionally upheld sex-based classifications, those have usually (not always) afforded some special benefit to females—such as a tax exemption for widows and not widowers, or a thirteen-year "up-or-out" period for female Navy lieutenants (unlike the nine-year period for males).[24] The spirit is of affirmative action for those disadvantaged or victimized by society.

Weinberger v. *Wiesenfeld*[25] overturned a provision of the Social Security Act paying certain survivors' benefits to both a widow and minor children in her care but to the children alone of a surviving widower. Justice Brennan manages to acknowledge that "the notion that men are more likely than women to be the primary supporters of their spouses and children" is not "entirely without empirical support." And he notes that the intent of Congress was to enable the surviving widow to remain at home to care for the children. These grudging concessions, however, only throw his conclusion into stark relief: the "gender-based distinction . . . is *entirely irrational*" (emphasis added). "It is no less important for a child to be cared for by its sole surviving parent when that parent is male rather than female." A father no less than a mother "has a right to remain at home caring and providing." As parents, father and mother are of equal capacity and equal rights; mothering and homemaking can be male as easily as female. This is true in some instances, and liberated minds may perceive it to be true in general. Most people deny it, however, and it will never be generally true. The trite truths so decried are nevertheless commonly true; the dogma of equality misses the singular ties normal between mother and the child she bears for months and can nourish for more months and the singular importance to most good families and homes of the mother's singular attention. Justices Lewis Powell and William Rehnquist concur in the result, agreeing that the discrimination is against the *families* of those who chanced to be principally male supported. But it is precisely the woman in the home that is the target of Justice Brennan's opinion for the Court.

Craig v. *Boren*, in 1976, showed how the principle of equal dignity overrides even differences whose relevance is admitted as well as obvious.[26] It overturned an Oklahoma law that distinguished the age at which males might purchase 3.2 percent beer (twenty-one) from the age for females (eighteen). Young males, Oklahoma argued, were far wilder with alcohol than young females. They were more than ten times as likely to be arrested for driving under the influence, for example. To appreciate Justice Brennan's grudging obfuscation of Oklahoma's evidence, one must peruse the opinion. He finally becomes somewhat forthright: "The principles embodied in the Equal Protection Clause are not to be rendered inapplicable" by "statistically measured" generalities, by "loose fitting generalities concerning the drinking tendencies of aggregate populations." Bluntly put, the principle of equal dignity is to prevail even in the face of the relevant and elemental inequalities between male and female that guided the state's attempt to reduce the dangers from young drinkers.

Stanton v. *Stanton* cuts more directly at the traditional American family.[27] It overturned a Utah law that established different ages of majority for males (twenty-one) and females (eighteen). In upholding the law, a Utah court had referred to some "old notions": that "generally it is the man's primary responsibility to provide a home and its essentials," "that it is then a salutary thing for him to get a good education and training," and "that girls tend generally to mature physically, emotionally, and mentally before boys." Justice Blackmun for the Supreme Court finesses the question of maturity. But he is determined to deny any special male superiority: "No longer is the female destined solely for the home and the rearing of the family, and only the male for the market place and the world of ideas." The "solely" surely exaggerates the historical problem. What of women's suffrage and the many colleges, universities, and opportunities long open to women?

Justice Blackmun supposes that the absence of full equality is a sign of systematic repression. Is it? Or might Justice Blackmun's outlook also be repressive, perhaps more repressive of inclination and happiness? The creed of equal dignity discourages females from respecting a special function as to children and home. While a special role need not be the only role for women of spirit, talent, and education, it is a great satisfaction for most women and an important contribution to their family and their country. But Justice Blackmun is preoccupied with inequality: "To distinguish between the two on educational grounds is to be self-serving: if the female is not to be supported so long as the male, she hardly can be expected to attend school as long as he does, and bringing her education to an end earlier coincides with the role-typing society has long imposed." We can disdain the old distinctions because they are artificially imposed by society and its culture. Individuals are to be liberated for their equality—and "society" is understood as just an artificial imposition of repressive pigeonholes. Who, however, will provide for society, not least for the good families that help form the characters, friendships, and associations so crudely homogenized and disguised by that modern abstraction "society"?

Taylor v. *Louisiana* exhibits the justices' bored disdain for such considerations.[28] A jury system in which women were selected only if they volunteered was held to deny the "representative cross-section" needed to satisfy due process. Justice White had to deal with a recent precedent that justified such a qualification because "woman is still regarded as the center of the home and family life,"[29] with Louisiana's attempt "to regulate and provide stability to the state's own idea of family life," and with the fact that Court and Congress had accepted all-male juries since the country began. His reply: "Communities differ at different times and places. What is a fair cross section at one time or place is not necessarily a fair cross section at another time or a different place." Role typing as practiced in Louisiana no longer deserves a serious reply.

I close with two cases of disparate subject and direction, which together illustrate the tension between prerequisites of family life and the permissive egalitarianism that largely influences the Court. *Belle Terre* v. *Boraas* shows a different way.[30] It upheld a village zoning ordinance that in effect excluded communes, fraternity houses, and the like. Equal protection, Justice William O. Douglas wrote for the Court, is not violated by a prohibition of all but one-family residences and of residency by more than two "unrelated" persons: "The police power is ample to lay out zones where family values, youth values, and the blessings of quiet seclusion, and clean air make the area a sanctuary for people." Justice Marshall alone dissented, citing the First Amendment's extended protections of self-expression. While zoning may distinguish use of land, it may not differentiate according to quality of people: "who those persons are, what they believe, or how they choose to live."

More characteristic, however, is *Department of Agriculture* v. *Moreno*, decided the previous year.[31] Justice Brennan's opinion (for seven justices) relies on a "freedom of association" derived from the First Amendment: Congress denied equal protection when it limited households eligible for food stamps to those whose members were related, thereby excluding hippies and communes.

Justice Brennan thus extended a principle Chief Justice Earl Warren had set forth and explained five years before. *King* v. *Smith*[32] overturned, as violating federal law and policy, the "man in the house" rule: a state regulation that excluded from federal assistance those children whose mothers have regular sexual relations with men not obliged to support their children. According to Chief Justice Warren, welfare policy now rests on a "basis considerably more sophisticated and enlightened than the " 'worthy person' concept" of earlier programs, which had attended to the moral quality of home life: "Immorality and illegitimacy should be dealt with through rehabilitative measures that do not punish dependent children, and . . . protection of such children is the paramount goal of AFDC [Aid to Families with Dependent Children]." Understandably compassionate toward the young, foolishly slighting the moral and social importance of worthy parents (or parent), the Court airily dismisses an incentive for preserving a sound family environment. It can do this complacently because of its faith in the progress of society and of social powers for "rehabilitation." Judges put responsibility for rectification upon a caring society just as they weaken the elemental society, the family, and the governor of society, the state and federal governments.

One must note the strange optimism. Chief Justice Warren supposes that the rather unpromising human beings often served will be cured of their personal and familial troubles by essentially voluntary "rehabilitative programs." To their credit and dignity, some can and will. Such successes are rather few. Changing habits is hard to do, people are now informed of their dignity whatever their life style, government is encouraged to remake people by carrots alone, and the Court limits its ability even to ration carrots. This case, after all, is about distribution of benefits, not imposition of punishments. Chief Justice Warren insists on new habits and attitudes by governmental prescription, just as his Court deprives government of one strong instrument, the withholding of cold cash, for encouraging even the merely external actions that it might reasonably expect.

Equal Dignity and Constitutional Government

While recent Supreme Courts advance the new agenda under this or that constitutional authorization, they transform the provisions they touch. What are the likely consequences for liberal or constitutional government?

The obvious effect has been much noticed: the demise of constitutional forms before the new priority of judicially mandated social policy. The new liberalism suspects constitutionalism to be intertwined with eighteenth-century notions of private rights and limited government. Its adherents are masters at finding why they cannot follow or find the original meaning of the Constitution. Supposing instead that they can find and follow moral evolution, thinking themselves morally superior to the old constitutionalists, judges of such a persuasion transform the old constraints. But a transforming evolution is a revolution. The new agenda takes the Constitution out of constitutional law.

The most obvious practical effect, also much noticed, is the confrontation of the political branches with the new powers of judges and of the administrators who execute judicial mandates. New authorities and priorities compete with the old powers and priorities: a presidential executive oriented to defense, civil order, and economic growth and security and a Congress largely reflecting a middle-class majority in its diverse groupings and diverse wealth.

The original Constitution had given a rather clear priority to Congress and president, to political rather than judicial authority. The Preamble suggests other aims of government besides justice—tranquillity, defense, the general welfare, and the blessings of liberty. For the establishment of justice, as well as the other aims, the first necessity was a government at once republican and institutionalized. Thus the new system might be popular and safe, on the one hand, and vested with the necessary powers, legislative, executive, and judicial, on the other. Justice would depend principally on politics in both American senses: the management of the electorate and the management of government. Instead of an active people, the new liberalism encourages one to be cared for by administrators prodded by activists; instead of political parties linking people and leaders, it fosters judicial mandates and administrative ministering.

In the original constitutionalism courts were to guard the Constitution, by the special American power of judicial review, and to protect individual rights, by the proper judicial function. Neither of these judicial powers was thought by its proponents to be political in the sense that the legislative and the executive were. Guarding the Constitution meant following the law, and if one had to go beyond it to interpret it, the judge was to look to the rights and powers, the natural or higher private and public law, implicit in constitutionalism. Nor did protection of rights amount to social or political policy. The spirit of rights was solicitude for private security, as by protecting the right of habeas corpus or of freedom of religion. *Marbury* v. *Madison*, which affirmed the doctrine that it is for judges to decide when "a right has vested," also distinguished sharply the "legal questions" that judges decide from the "political questions" reserved to the discretion of legislature and executive.[33] The modern reforming judge, in contrast, smiles at the political questions doctrine and disdains the old lines between law and politics. A complacent faith in social progress, however, blinds him to the harm he may do to an intricately arranged political system.

Still, it will be objected that a modern interdependent society breaks down any sharp distinction between private and public. One can add that even the old judicial protection of private security and freedom revolutionized society. It promoted "society" in its first modern sense: the network of commercial dealings among private individuals who are hard working, entrepreneurial, rather tolerant, intolerant of caste or slavery, rather earnest, and respectable in familial, social, and sexual mores. The reformers of our time are indignant at this modern middle class's superiority and respectability, believe in liberation and social policy, and disdain the lines between private and social. Again, however, the presumption that liberation and caring will bring social progress often hides the actual wounds inflicted on society. That is the argument of this paper. The wounds are to good families, decent upbringing, and moral education and to the kind of populace, also planned by the old liberal philosophers and statesmen, that sustains a constitutional republic.

The principle of equal dignity encourages universal compassion for all persons, whatever their contributions to themselves, their children, or their fellow citizens. Self-expression as persons is the watchword, not self-reliance as individuals and self-government as citizens. Self-expression involves the so-called authentic self, a unique and impassioned persona. "Question authority" is the paradoxically authoritative maxim of this outlook. A free citizen, however, must respect what is good for free government, in particular those authorities, such as the Constitution and laws, that foster political self-government and moral self-government. As the new spirit erases loyalties to all established institutions and principles, however, it elevates the authority of unrepresentative courts and intellectuals and of the creed of equal liberation. Intolerance grows, in the form of an amoral moralism that insists that every lifestyle, especially those previously discriminated against, must be tolerated.

In fact, the new creed is part of a social movement that causes a revamped public, a reformed people in the political sense. There arise associations and organizations of those disadvantaged by social status or social attitude, whose power and enfranchisement the judiciary often directly aids. Corresponding to these, often instigating them, are activist patrons on congressional committees, in public interest groups, the universities and the law schools, and especially in the omnipresent media, themselves under the patronage of a judicially expanded First Amendment. These groupings amount to the distinctively modern parts of the Democratic party in its post–New Deal liberal coalition. They are the activist and public-spirited elements of the revamped public.

Yet their creed encourages something else in the majority: a mass of rather hollow men and women, heterogeneous only superficially, reluctant to govern themselves, eager to blame society for their ills, and taught to expect a continuous warm bath of approval and satisfaction. They incline to personal indulgence, which they regard as their right, and are cynical about duty and commitment, which seem rationalizations of a repressive and alienating system. They encourge political institutions to become either conduits for popular demands, instruments overloaded but not authoritative, or nonpolitical providers of services, administrative instruments increasingly expanded and inefficient.

Such tendencies exacerbate the centralized institutions and peculiarly individual loneliness to which liberal societies incline, especially after their economies have been redirected from the primacy of production and the right to acquire property toward the primacy of consumerism and the freedoms from want and fear. One must also note new kinds of dangers from ungoverned passions and the violence of a liberated underclass. Tentacles of licentiousness and criminality expand as the new fashions undermine and intimidate churches, old pieties, parochial loyalties, sexual morals, marriage, firm upbringing, the police, and the neighborhood. Those called "disadvantaged," as if society can be held responsible for their fate, are in this respect further disadvantaged by their more egalitarian and libertarian patrons. We should not be surprised if they, or perhaps the baffled but dominant middle class, turn in a crisis to violence or to unscrupulous leaders who are willing to act altogether outside of a constitutional system now disdained by even the legal establishment that was to protect it.

Much now depends on what happens on the bench and within the law schools. It is a truism of political science, going back to its founder, that the friend of democracy should encourage not what is most democratic but what most helps democracy to endure. For a liberal democracy it is a maxim especially appropriate when a new liberalism corrodes constitutional government, as well as simple justice.

Notes

1. "The Constitution of the United States: Contemporary Ratification," *The Great Debate: Interpreting Our Written Constitution* (Washington, D.C.: Federalist Society, 1986), p. 18.

2. Richard E. Morgan, *Disabling America* (New York: Basic Books, 1984); Macklin Fleming, *The Price of Perfect Justice* (New York: Basic Books, 1974); Lino A. Graglia, *Disaster by Decree* (Ithaca, N.Y.: Cornell University Press, 1976). But see Stanley C. Brubaker, "Mainstream Nihilism," *Commentary,* vol. 86 (December 1986), pp. 36–42.

3. "Constitution of the United States: Contemporary Ratification," p. 18.

4. Ibid., p. 22.

5. Ibid., pp. 11, 20.

6. Martin Luther King, Jr., *Why We Can't Wait* (New York: New American Library, 1964), p. vi.

7. Yick Wu v. Hopkins, 118 US 356, 370 (1886).

8. Eisenstadt v. Baird, 405 US 438, 440–55 (1972).

9. Griswold v. Connecticut, 381 US 479 (1965).

10. Douglas J. Besharov and Alison J. Quin, "Not All Female-Headed Families Are Created Equal," *Public Interest,* vol. 89 (Fall 1987), p. 55.

11. Mary Ann Glendon, *Abortion and Divorce in Western Law* (Cambridge, Mass.: Harvard University Press, 1987).

12. Ibid., p. 2

13. Ibid., p. 55.

14. Ibid., p. 24.

15. Stanley v. Georgia, 394 US 557, 558–68 (1969).

16. Stanley v. Georgia, 394 US 557, 567 (1969).

17. Bowers v. Hardwick (dissenting opinion), 106 S.Ct. 2841 (1986), at 2853.

18. Miller v. California, 413 US 15, 16–37 (1973); Paris Adult Theater I v. Slaton, 413 US 49, 50–70 (1973).

19. Young v. American Mini-Theaters, 427 US 50, at 61 (1975); see also Renton v. Playtime Theaters, Inc., 475 US 41 (1986).

20. Bowers v. Hardwick, 106 S.Ct. 2841 (1986).

21. Labine v. Vincent, 401 US 532 (1971), Court opinion 533–40, Harlan's opinion 540, Brennan's opinion 541–59.

22. Weber v. Aetna Cas & Sur Co, 406 US 164 (1972); Stanley v. Illinois, 405 US 645 (1972); see also Trimble v. Gordon, 430 US 762 (1976).

23. Frontiero v. Richardson, 411 US 677, 678–91, at 684, 686 (1973).

24. Kahn v. Shevin, 416 US 351, 352–56 (1974); Schlesinger v. Ballard, 419 US 498, 499–510 (1975).

25. Weinberger v. Wiesenfeld, 420 US 636 (1975).

26. Craig v. Boren, 429 US 190 (1976).

27. Stanton v. Stanton, 421 US 7 (1975).

28. Taylor v. Louisiana, 419 US 522 (1974).

29. Hoyt v. Florida, 368 US 57, at 68 (1961). The argument continues: "We cannot say that it is constitutionally permissible for a state, acting in pursuit of the general welfare, to conclude that a woman should be relieved from the

civic duty of jury service unless she herself determines that such service is consistent with her own special responsibilities."

30. Belle Terre v. Boraas, 416 US 1, 2–9 (1974).
31. Department of Agriculture v. Moreno, 413 US 528, 529–38 (1973).
32. King v. Smith, 392 US 309, 311–34 (1968).
33. Marbury v. Madison, 1 Cranch 137 (1803).

7
Constitutional Interpretation and Regime Principles

Harry M. Clor

The Constitution tells us, in the Preamble, that to "establish justice" is one of the grand purposes of the document. What kind of justice? How and by whom are its precepts to be ascertained? To what extent, or in what sense, are they discernible in the written Constitution? Nowadays, to raise such questions is, almost unavoidably, to become enmeshed in that remarkably intense and intensifying conflict over the role and limits of judicial power—the controversy over judicial activism and democratic government.

In recent debate on this subject, the battle lines have been drawn rather sharply. According to the so-called interpretivists, constitutional adjudication must be confined to norms discoverable in the document, and a textual norm must be construed rigorously in accordance with the original intention of the men who framed and ratified it. Those who go by the name of noninterpretivists maintain that judges necessarily create constitutional law and that they may and ought to do so on the basis of contemporary social values or ideas of right. The main consequences of the latter view are that rights-conferring clauses (freedom of speech, equal protection, and so on) are construed quite expansively and that new personal rights are created (for example, a general right of privacy). That, the interpretivist retorts, is intolerable judicial aggrandizement in derogation of majority rule or popular government—the essence of our democracy. To this the noninterpretivist is inclined to reply that the rights of the individual (or human rights), against the state and the majority, are the essence of our polity. Furthermore, broad constitutional generalities affirming these rights are to be defined by the adjudicator in light of the best present-day moral theory. Hence constitutional rights are enlarged and new ones established on the basis of current doctrines of equality, personal autonomy, and, above all, "human dignity." In opposition to these consequences the interpretivist is inclined to denigrate moral and political theory, denying it any legitimate role in constitutional interpretation. On this view, what constitutional provisions mean is to be determined largely by inquiries into historical records bearing on the objectives of their originators. As for justice, the interpretivists (when they speak of it at all) tend to identify it with popular rule or the consent of the governed; the noninterpretivists (who speak of it often) tend to identify it with rights as understood by contemporary egalitarian and libertarian thought.

Sketchy though it is, this overview should serve to make credible the following observations about the controversy. Contrary to what their names might logically suggest, interpretivism and noninterpretivism do not necessarily exhaust possible approaches to the import of the United States Constitution. While interesting arguments are made on both sides of this dispute, neither perspective is entirely satisfying as a determinative horizon for thinking about constitutional law. Further, more is at stake here than the appropriate role and limits of judicial power. In significant respects this is a dispute about the nature of the Constitution and of the political regime it is designed to promote. Although this fact is often obscured by the terms in which the debate is conducted, what is ultimately at stake is whether our traditional understanding of republican or liberal government will be replaced by a new understanding.

The theses of this essay can be briefly summarized. If, as I believe, it is important to preserve our republican constitutional order against certain more or less radical jurisprudential innovations, one must conclude that the interpretivist approach is insufficient for the purpose. An effective jurisprudence of moderation has to be informed by a kind of constitutional wisdom that is not entirely separable from wisdom about civic fundamentals. Finally, in our civic fundamentals, and therefore in the "spirit" of the Constitution, moderation and justice are associated.

The Principles Underlying the Constitution

American attitudes toward the nature and function of courts of law have always been infused with a kind of duality. On the one hand we have recognized the Supreme Court as a political institution, an authority involved in governing. On the other hand we have viewed courts as legal tribunals, devoted to the application of established law, constrained by elaborate procedural formalities, and constituting an impersonal forum for recourse to politically neutral rules. These two representations of our legal world need not be mutually exclusive, but they become so when each is carried to its utmost extremity.

These perpectives are encompassed, though unequally, in Alexander Hamilton's classic justification for judicial review in the seventy-eighth *Federalist* paper. Hamilton goes to considerable lengths to depict the federal courts as ordinary courts of law subject to all the customary rules and usages that have defined the judicial task. Hence "they should be bound down by strict rules and precedents" and rendered politically independent so that "nothing would be consulted but the Constitution and the laws."[1] But there is another, if less prominent, theme. A branch of government holding the position of "an intermediate body between the people and the legislature," periodically restraining them both, cannot really be regarded as a politically insignificant institution.[2] Moreover, Hamilton does not mean, literally, that the judges are expected to consult nothing but the Constitution and the laws. He suggests that the judicial magistracy will have an important duty to perform in mitigating or limiting the operation of unjust and partial laws that might not be unconstitutional.[3] It would seem, then, that the "courts of justice" were expected to have in view certain standards of right that are not necessarily to be found in the written Constitution.

A similar duality can be seen in the work of Chief Justice John Marshall. The line of argument establishing judicial review in *Marbury* v. *Madison* rests on the premise that the Constitution is a body of *law,* therefore to be expounded by judges whose business is legal judgment (and not merely a collection of civic admonitions that could be expounded just as well or better by the political branches of government).[4] But *McCulloch* v. *Maryland* makes it clear that the Constitution is no ordinary body of law.[5] The heart of Marshall's argument there on behalf of implied powers is the sharp distinction he makes between a legal code, which is a body of detailed and immutable *rules,* and a constitution, whose "nature, therefore, requires that only its great outlines should be marked, its important objects designated, and the minor ingredients [like a national bank!] which compose those objects be deduced from the nature of the objects themselves."[6] Interesting questions are raised here about the nature of the judgment that the Court is making when it decides that a legislative act is or is not compatible with those "great outlines" and "important objects" that characterize the Constitution.

As everyone knows, Marshall's characterization of the Constitution is calculated to preclude an alternative view of it that would have the Constitution dictate for all times and circumstances the means by which government may exercise the powers granted to it. "Let the end be legitimate, let it be within the scope of the Constitution, and all means which are appropriate, which are plainly adapted to that end, which are not prohibited, but consistent with the letter and spirit of the Constitution are constitutional."[7] This renowned formulation

117

conceptualizes the problem of constitutional judgment largely in terms of means and ends, and it treats the latter as the decisive factor. The Court has to determine the legitimacy of the end Congress seeks to achieve, and this presupposes that the Constitution, properly construed, provides a teaching about the legitimate ends of government. But how in the constitutional text alone is such a teaching to be found? The document lists certain powers of the national government, such as the power to regulate commerce, and the Preamble presents a list of ends that the Constitution aspires to promote. But neither the powers nor the great objectives of the Preamble are defined or explicitly articulated in the document.

This is a subject on which it is vital to avoid misunderstandings. I am not suggesting that Marshall ever embraced the doctrine of a boundlessly flexible and adaptable Constitution. For Marshall the great outlines and important objects are permanent realities by which adjudication can and should be guided. But to receive such guidance one must reflect on the Constitution as a whole and with a view to its "spirit" or its purposes. The purposes are political and ethical considerations, and effective reflection on them cannot very well be confined to what is, so to speak, clearly inside the constitutional text. When we consider *Marbury* and *McCulloch* together, we can scarcely avoid the perplexing question, What does it mean to interpret a Constitution like ours?—a Constitution that is law but also extraordinary law whose relatively indefinite provisions point to political fundamentals. From the beginning it was virtually inevitable that courts would have to seek guidance from political and ethical realities transcending the constitutional text.

Such judicial appeals to transcendent considerations abound in our constitutional law. Chief Justice Marshall accomplished this on a number of occasions, most obviously in *Fletcher* v. *Peck*,[8] which rests rather heavily on an appeal to "general principles [of property] which are common to our free institutions."[9] Another outstanding example is Justice Benjamin Cardozo's employment of the concept of "ordered liberty" in *Palko* v. *Connecticut*.[10] There are less familiar but equally interesting instances of the phenomenon. *Reynolds* v. *United States*, upholding antipolygamy statutes against claims of religious freedom, relied in part on our national commitment to the monogamous family as an indispensable support for a republican regime.[11] The written Constitution says nothing about the family. In *Pierce* v. *Society of Sisters* the Court read the Fourteenth Amendment's due process clause as affirming the right of parents to send their children to a private school.[12] The Court said: "The fundamental theory of liberty upon which all governments in this Union repose excludes any general power of the state to standardize its children by forcing them to accept instruction from public teachers only. The child is not the mere creature of the state."[13] This theory of liberty is not exactly discoverable in the constitutional text; the Court supposes, however, that it is discoverable in practices and premises underlying our constitutional order.

Multitudes of additional cases could be offered to illustrate the point, but the ones cited are notable for several reasons. They span a long period of time in our constitutional history antedating our current debates over constitutional interpretation. They have been generally respected among supporters of judicial sobriety. Their results are diverse: two of them uphold claims of right against the state (*Fletcher* and *Pierce*), while the other two reject claims of personal right on behalf of civic order or public morality (*Palko* and *Reynolds*). And, once again, they all rely on ethical or political desiderata located somewhere beyond the written Constitution. While those desiderata are not the sole determinants of the decision in cases such as these, it would be relatively easy to show that they are vital components of the reasoning process by which constitutional conclusions are reached and defended as valid.

Is this widespread judicial practice entirely unjustified? The practice is justifiable (in some of its instances) on a view of what it means to regard the Constitution as an organic instrument whose parts are frequently in need of illumination from reflection on the whole. Thinking about the Constitution as a whole ultimately entails inquiry about the kind of political society it is designed to promote. (Doesn't it?) One begins to discern an order of principles, ends, and institutions to be subserved—a "regime." For example, "federalism" is nowhere described in the constitutional text, but it is a political structure implied in the constitutional design. Likewise, "freedom of association" is nowhere mentioned in the document, but almost everyone thinks that the Constitution somehow entails such a principle (liberals think so in First Amendment cases and conservatives in Fourteenth Amendment "state action" cases).

To put the point a bit differently, the Constitution belongs to American liberal democracy, and the import of many of its provisions cannot be grasped without reference to basic ideas and concerns of liberal democracy. There is then an inevitable connection between constitutional norms and the norms of the American polity. Two brief illustrations will have to suffice. The legal meaning of "equal protection of the laws" must depend, in part, on consideration of the American idea of equality—an idea of equal civic rights associated with an aspiration to equality of opportunity (as distinguished from

119

substantive or material equality). The scope and limits of "the free-dom of speech" have to be determined with a view to the reasons for a free speech principle in our kind of democracy. None of this is to say that the constitutional text is a blank slate or that there is an "unwrit-ten constitution" in authority over the written one. It is to say that constitutional provisions entail, and point to, a certain vision of civil society and of right that is not (because it could not be) fully articu-lated in the text.

Critics will object that this conceptualization of what constitu-tionality means raises more questions and problems than it resolves. The objection has some merit. After all, the meaning of regime princi-ples like liberty, equality, or property may be in dispute, and their bearing on particular cases is still more often in dispute. The judg-ments called for (especially in hard cases) are difficult and sometimes quite delicate ones. But let us see how well interpretivist jurispru-dence can avoid these difficulties and, to the extent that it avoids them, at what cost.

The Limits of Interpretivist Jurisprudence

An unqualifiedly interpretivist position—what might be called pure or hard-line interpretivism—would confine constitutional inquiry to the specific clause (or clauses) bearing on the case at hand. The meaning of a constitutional clause would be identical with the specific intention of its framers. If, as Raoul Berger claims, we can determine from the recorded debates of the Thirty-ninth Congress that the authors of the Fourteenth Amendment aimed *only* to constitutionalize the limited body of rights accorded Negroes by the Civil Rights Act of 1866, that and only that is what the Fourteenth Amendment means.[14] It follows that in *Brown* v. *Board of Education* (and most other decisions of the twentieth century) the Supreme Court could only have been acting as a "continuing constitutional convention," imposing its opin-ions on our elected representatives contrary to the rule of law and the democratic principle.[15]

Taken literally, this approach makes the act of constitutional judgment essentially a matter of research into legislative archives and such historical circumstances as may illuminate the data therein. It tends to reduce the Constitution itself to a collection of particular objectives, discernment of which has nothing to do with any judg-ments about justice and injustice. Surely neither the Court nor the American public has ever understood constitutional law quite as narrowly as this. If, as Tocqueville and others have remarked, in the United States great political issues tend to become constitutional issues, that must be on account of a national view of what constitutionality means more comprehensive than what is offered by hard-line interpretivists.[16] And we may at least surmise that our national reverence for the Constitution has depended on the more comprehensive view.

Many proponents of the interpretivist position, especially (and interestingly) sitting judges, seem to find the doctrine in its pure form hard to live with. Hence we encounter various modifying versions of the doctrine, amounting to a shift of the adjudicative focus (somewhat) away from the *specific* intentions. In one formula or another a distinction is made between the particular aims that the framers of a provision had in view, which are sometimes called their "immediate expectations," and the basic idea or "core principle" that they embodied in the provision. When circumstances so dictate, the former can be made to give way to the latter—which is, after all, what really counts. On this basis one may argue, for example, that *Brown* v. *Board* was rightly decided even though the Thirty-ninth Congress never had either segregation or schools in mind; in light of subsequent experience we can clearly see that segregated schooling violates the Fourteenth Amendment's underlying idea of racial equality. Of course, this is truly an interpretivist approach only insofar as the underlying or core principle articulated (by the court or commentator) is in fact the one that the framers intended.

In a notably temperate formulation of the position, Judge Robert Bork says:

> All that an intentionalist requires is that the text, structure and history of the Constitution provide him not with a conclusion but with a premise. That premise states a value that the framers intended to protect. The intentionalist judge must then supply the minor premise in order to protect the constitutional freedom in circumstances the framers could not foresee.[17]

Judge Bork apparently acknowledges that in *applying* the premise to present circumstances (for example, supplying the "minor premise" that electronic media should be covered by the First Amendment's free speech clause) the court has to exercise a discretionary judgment. But the interesting questions are about the identification of the basic premise. For Bork the judge's task here is to "discern a principle" amidst the (perhaps outdated) particulars that the framers had in view, and in so doing the problem is to decide at what level of abstraction or generality that principle is to be articulated.[18] Is the basic premise of the Fourteenth Amendment simply a precept about

121

the equal status of black people? Or is it, more generally, about racial equality? Or is it a still more comprehensive principle encompassing all persons? Bork's response to this dilemma is that "the problem of levels of generality is solved by choosing no level of generality higher than that which interpretation of the words, structure and history of the Constitution fairly supports."[19] Decisive for that resolution is the historical evidence concerning what was and was not under discussion when the amendment was proposed and ratified.

The question arises whether a solution to the problem of levels of generality (assuming that the attitudes of the framers *and ratifiers* are clear enough to provide one) is sufficient to establish what a constitutional clause means. Supposing that Bork's adjudicator is reasonably persuaded that racial equality and nothing else was under discussion, that by itself does not fully determine the content of the principle. What idea or vision of racial equality? Is it, for instance, one that would be compatible or incompatible with affirmative action programs? Why, exactly, would it preclude a genuinely "equal but separate" treatment of the races?

If problems of interpretation are presented by the Fourteenth Amendment, for which we have a substantial legislative record, still larger ones are presented by the First Amendment's free speech clause, for which we do not. The debates of the First Congress reveal that attention was devoted to whether such a provision is necessary, but discusison bearing on the scope and limits of "the freedom of speech" is notoriously scarce. It makes sense to suppose that the First Congress agreed with its predecessor, the Continental Congress, that the freedom conduces to "the advancement of truth, science, morality and art in general," as well as "diffusion of liberal sentiments on administration of government" and popular surveillance of officeholders.[20] But, as to the actual intention of the provision, most research seems to support the contention of the Federalists (during the controversy over the Alien and Sedition acts) that it was meant to prohibit prior restraint of publication and nothing more.

If we are not to be governed by that construction—a position for which there are no contemporary advocates—then the core principle must be defined on some basis other than what historical research can tell us about the intent of the First Congress. In apparent defense of some of the expanded First Amendment adjudication of the twentieth century, Judge Bork has stated that "the entire structure of the Constitution creates a representative democracy, a form of government that would be meaningless without freedom to discuss government and its policies."[21] Presumably, "structure of the Constitution" does not refer simply to the will of those who enacted the First Amendment.

(Does it refer to the general free speech philosophy of the founding generation? or to prerequisites of a well-functioning liberal democracy?)

My point in all this is that the textual "premise" is not usually self-defining and that the task of defining it is seldom simply one of discovering an empirical fact—that thus-and-such a precept was in the minds of the framers. The premise has to be *formulated,* and much depends on the body of ideas that we bring to the enterprise. Since Judge Bork's approach requires adjudication to begin with a norm referred to in the text, it is serviceable as a restriction on judicial creation of comprehensive rights (like the privacy right) to which the written Constitution makes no reference whatever. What it cannot do, however, is conclusively preclude any need for judicial recourse to regime considerations.

It will be said that such appeals beyond the written Constitution violate the principle of the rule of law. Interpretivists argue that, whenever we find the original understanding of a textual provision inadequate for our concerns, the only democratic solution is the one the framers mandated: let the people decide on a constitutional amendment. Yet, as attention to their political theory indicates, the founders did not want to encourage frequent recourse to the public for the settlement of constitutional issues. As James Madison observed, frequent reference of constitutional matters to popular vote would result in such engagement of popular passions and such mutability of the Constitution as would undermine "reverence for the laws."[22]

In interpretivist thought the rule of law appears to mean conformity to the will of the original lawmakers until such time as the population formally expresses its will to the contrary. But we may doubt that this thoroughgoing identification of *law* and *will* is wholly in accord with the philosophy that presided over the establishment of our republic. The founders seem to have identified the rule of law, in part, with the stability and continuity of wisely developed legal norms. To be under "the rule of law not men" one should have, to borrow from Lockean terminology, "a standing rule to live by," and that has to include some longstanding precepts.[23] That this rule of law mandates a restraint on the popular (as well as the judicial) will is a consideration in which contemporary interpretivism does not manifest much interest. At any rate, from the system the founders established there devolves on the Supreme Court a crucial responsibility: to elaborate constitutional norms in view of changing circumstances and to do so in such a way as to preserve the stability and continuity of the law.

In another respect a strictly interpretivist approach can be seen as an inadequate guide to the understanding and preservation of our established constitutional polity. Focusing adjudication as narrowly as it does on particular clauses and the particular wills of their authors, this jurisprudence tends to neglect—or place out of constitutional bounds—any broad consideration of the prerequisites of a healthy liberal democracy. Walter Berns finds fault with the recent Supreme Court, which "tends to expand the rights of republican citizenship but ignore altogether . . . its conditions or preconditions."[24] What Berns is talking about are moral preconditions—requisites of public spiritedness, civility, and moderation. By striking down most efforts of the states to support civic virtue (through support of private agencies like the family and religion in which decent habits are generated), the Court has unleashed "immoderate" interests contrary to the needs of "a republican regime."[25] But how are such needs and concerns cognizable by a jurisprudence that looks only to the objects that the authors of specific provisions had in mind? How many constitutional clauses were written and approved with a view to promoting the virtues (as distinguished from the rights) of citizens?

Arguably, some of those qualities of character called virtues or decency are presupposed by the written Constitution, but they are not mentioned in it. One can find attention devoted to them in some Supreme Court opinions. The connection between monogamous marriage and republicanism is recognized in *Reynolds* v. *United States*.[26] Even recently, in *Paris Adult Theater* v. *Slaton*, the claims of public decency are defended against pornography (obliquely, perhaps, since the claims of public decency are referred to as "the quality of life").[27] Reasonings of this sort, however, are hardly judicial reasonings in the strict interpretivist mold. Courts must be able to transcend that mold if *moral preconditions* of liberal democracy are to receive the recognition that many conservatives and moderates (including, surely, some interpretivists) insist they should have.[28] Insofar as the conservation of traditional institutions and standards, as well as popular rule, is an animating concern of interpretivist thought, it must be said that its means are insufficient for its ends.

Noninterpretivist Ideas of Justice

The conservation of traditional institutions and standards is evidently no animating concern of noninterpretivist doctrines. They are, for the most part, strikingly present-oriented or forward-looking doctrines. With more candor than most noninterpretivist writers, Michael Perry maintains that the ideal constitutional adjudicator "resolves moral problems not simply by looking backward to the sediment of old moralities, but ahead to the emergent principles in terms of which fragments of a new moral order can be forged."[29] By what authority do nonelected judges become leading participants in the forging of a new moral order? The authority relied on is that of current, politically progressive moral and religious philosophy. Little effort is required to discern the ideological direction of the emergent principles (concerning "distributive justice and the role of government, freedom of political dissent, racism and sexism, the death penalty, human sexuality") that Perry would have constitutionalized.[30] Almost by definition, these could not be our fundamental regime principles, since their virtue is supposed to lie in their transformative potential. By what right may nonelected judges aim to promote a regime transformation?

In support of contemporary progressive jurisprudence, the ultimate appeal is to a concept of justice. In the various formulations of that concept one discerns a central idea—that all persons have, or are entitled to, "equal dignity." This dignity principle, as we may call it, is generally advanced as a categorical ethical and constitutional norm, taking precedence over all political desiderata or standards of value that may be in competition with its demands. The principle is invoked far more often than it is defined.[31] When the idea is articulated, it is in terms such as these: that every human being has intrinsic worth, that all persons must be treated equally, as ends rather than means, and that the respect due to the individual as a moral agent entails a personal right to full autonomy in the choice of a way of life.

The dignity principle has two striking implications. First of all, it is probably the most powerful energizer of judicial activism that one could envision. The idea expresses a moral imperative that is both unconditional and virtually limitless in its scope. What, after all, are the outer limits of each person's compelling claim to be treated in accordance with the equal intrinsic worth of every human being?

Second, the dignity principle, as employed by its advocates, reflects a doctrinal viewpoint that is not exactly universal; it is a prolific generator of individual rights—of a certain sort. In the area of criminal law it is obviously employed to weight the scales of justice rather heavily on the side of those accused of wrongdoing. And when courts seek to weigh claims on behalf of public morality against claims on behalf of individual self-expression or life style (as in obscenity, public vulgarity, and "privacy" cases), the principle tips the scales so much in favor of the latter as virtually to preclude any weighing at all.[32]

The ideological character and consequent one-sidedness of this concept are probably best illustrated by the legal philosophy of Ronald Dworkin. In his version of the concept, the state is morally required to treat every person with "equal concern and respect." Unlike Perry, Dworkin does not acknowledge the innovative character of his precept; he maintains that it reflects the authentic liberal (hence American) idea of justice. To establish the primacy of that idea, Dworkin sets out to refute the widespread opinion that there are conflicts between equality and liberty calling for compromise and that private property is a component of liberty deserving recognition. This view is dismissed because "in any strong sense of right, which would be competitive with the right to equality, there exists no general right to liberty at all."[33] What exist are certain kinds of liberties—freedom of expression and personal life style—that derive from everyone's fundamental right to equality of concern and respect. These liberties are entitled to the most stringent constitutional protection, while private property is without entitlement because it is not entailed by the basic principle of equality. Moreover, "those who have less talent, as the [economic] market judges talent, have a right to some form of redistribution in the name of justice."[34] The theory of justice expressed here is clearly that of John Rawls: "undeserved" natural disadvantages are to be redressed by the community as a matter of right.[35] Rawls recognizes that his prescriptions mandate a society rather different from the one we have been living in. The upshot of the Rawls-Dworkin prescriptions is a polity that is morally obliged to redistribute the wealth and employ "remedial" racial quotas but need not recognize property rights and may not prohibit polygamy or pornography.

A strictly interpretivist response to the dignity principle—that we cannot find it in the constitutional text—is not enough. In the long run, a jurisprudence that confines itself to a relatively legalistic mode of argument would be hard pressed to counter a jurisprudence that appeals to seemingly compelling ideas of the just society.

Justice and the Constitution

The understanding of justice informing the establishment of our republic can be briefly summarized thus: government by consent of the governed that is so designed as to protect the equal natural rights of all to life, liberty, and the pursuit of happiness. Since the majority of the governed might unwisely withhold consent from measures necessary for the protection of those rights or even sanction the abuse of some of them, an ethical tension is endemic to the theory and practice of our polity. We are all familiar with the political arrangements by which the founders sought to resolve or reduce the tension: numerous checks and balances, federalism, representative institutions able to "refine and enlarge the public views," and, finally, power-restricting constitutional provisions supported by judicial review and public respect for lawfulness.[36] Balances of power, among governmental agencies and among economic interests as well, were supposed to ensure that popular measures threatening to individual rights would at least be subject to debate and modification.

Yet the founders were aware that there is such a thing as excessive emphasis on rights; the *Federalist* asserts that "liberty may be endangered by the abuses of liberty as well as by the abuses of power."[37] Hence the Bill of Rights that Congress finally proposed to the states was a considerably more modest, less far-reaching compendium of liberties than what many state conventions had demanded under the influence of libertarian Anti-Federalists.[38] We may say that, while the founders sought to accommodate the desiderata of majority rule and individual rights, they were not majoritarian populists, nor were they subscribers to that brand of libertarian doctrine for which "rights against the state" is what the public good is all about.

The arrangements of the constituted regime were, in the words of an eminent scholar, "an attempt to institutionalize moderation."[39] The result was a balanced republic whose various balances should be (and normally are) understood as ingredients of American justice. Underlying the whole system is a rather sober view of human nature: human beings are, for the most part, creatures of self-interest; nobility is seldom to be expected; passion, when unchecked, usually prevails over reason.

The majoritarian enthusiasm of some interpretivists might be tempered by attention to the nonpopulist side of the founding philosophy. But we are primarily concerned here with the rights enthusiasts and their idea of equal dignity. Our original theory of justice differs from the Rawlsian and Dworkinian theory of it in several ways. As usually employed, the dignity principle scarcely recognizes that there are two sides to the problem of justice—that the "consent of the governed," as well as personal rights, is an imperative of liberal justice. Furthermore, the old and the new ideas differ substantially as to the character of the rights that are to be secured. Nowhere in our historic civic philosophy is there any suggestion of a right to have one's choice of life style (whatever it may be) respected by the community as much as anyone else's choice of life style. The respect due to citizens from the state has (until recently) never meant equal status and autonomy for all ways of life that persons may happen to prefer. Nor is there any suggestion in natural rights theory that those less favored in the "natural lottery" of talents are entitled to material compensation exacted from the resources of those more favored. On the contrary, that principle is highly problematic in light of property rights explicitly recognized in the Constitution, justified in the Lockean theory lying behind it, and elaborated in Marshallian and subsequent jurisprudence. The doctrine of natural rights is silent about the proper distribution of the material goods of this world, mandating an egalitarian policy no more than a policy of reward according to virtue. Within limits that I have alluded to, it leaves the people's representatives free to opt for more or less of a welfare state, as, within limits, it leaves us (collectively) free to decide among alternative policies toward public morality and criminal justice.

In other words, classical natural rights theory, unless distorted by misinterpretation, allows a considerable latitude for practical, prudential judgment on matters contingent and changeable. It also allows latitude for the exercise of ethical judgments above and beyond its prescriptions. We may choose to adopt a standard of equality of opportunity, involving assistance to the poor and the disabled, that is not dictated to us by natural or constitutional right. Likewise, we may adopt standards of public decency or retributive justice that are not so dictated.

The new moral philosophy is more imperious. The "dignity rights" are more extensive than the old ones; the far-reaching moral demands and prohibitions that they place on the community are harder to reconcile with majority rule (as with other aspects of the public good). Arguably, the American Constitution is not meant to guarantee a wholly just and desirable society (on anyone's conception thereof); it is meant to guarantee certain elemental political and ethical conditions.[40] Those elemental conditions that are called rights have the character of (equal) immunities from arbitrary power rather than entitlements to resources; overall, their aim is to provide opportunities rather than fulfillments. The constitutional philosophy, encompassing more desiderata than these rights, will sometimes encourage, without obliging, the legislator to go beyond them. While more is envisioned in that philosophy than what is manifest in the text, there is no suggestion in it of an aspiration to constitutionalize everything that wisdom might find to be good and just.

As for the role of the judiciary, the enumeration of rights, and their adjudication, is only one of the several devices by which the Constitution seeks to "establish justice." As I have implied, it is by no means the most important device. Our constitution makers reasonably believed that the security of liberty depends, ultimately and most profoundly, on the structure of the government, especially well-balanced representative institutions, and on the character of the society, especially that diversity of economic and social interests that a commercial society tends to generate.[41] Therefore, it would be most incorrect to say that the Constitution establishes justice primarily by having the precepts of justice articulated and affirmed in federal courts. The function of the Supreme Court in the articulation and affirmation of our regime principles is a subordinate one.

The Principles of Our Civic Order

I have been arguing, however, that our system does leave room for such a function. The argument has been that, when it is necessary to go beyond the language of a constitutional provision and the objectives of its authors, the Court may look to, but never transcend or transform, the established principles of our civic order. How does one undertake to determine what those principles are?

Surely they cannot be grasped without serious attention to our past. And in our past the founding and the ideas presiding over it are of special importance for the adjudicative task. Why that special importance? Unlike most of the world's polities, the United States was deliberately established. At the beginning we affirmed the principles and purposes of the enterprise, deliberated systematically about the character of our union, and generated a rationale, both theoretical and practical, for our institutions. To a remarkable extent the institutions are still intact and continue to serve the purposes for which they were designed. In vital respects we still live in the liberal commercial republic that the founders envisioned. Therefore, the original rationale continues to be crucial to our self-understanding. Moreover, we have no other rationale that is both comprehensive and authoritatively constituted among us. (The competing Rawlsian theory can lay claim to comprehensiveness, but it does not give an account of *our* institutions and way of life, nor has it any public authorization to do so.) Hence those who wish to understand the Constitution of the United States are missing much if they look to the deliberations of, say, the Constitutional Convention or the First Congress only for what they can tell us about the intention (or intentions) of the men who wrote a constitutional clause—as if the point is to discover an antecedent will that we have to obey. There is a larger reason for looking to the perspective of the founding period. One wants to learn about the premises of the constitutional polity in which we live— thereby to recover the wisdom that has made it a successful preserver of decent liberty. If this were not so, why would the intentions of the framers merit such authoritative status now as is claimed for them?

The philosophy of the founding, however, cannot be the sole legitimate source for an understanding of the constitutional polity. Certainly there are occasions when it is an insufficient guide. The insufficiency has several causes; one of them is alteration introduced by constitutional amendment. The Fourteenth Amendment is not the only exemplar of this factor, but it is an important one. However limited its specific intentions may have been, surely the amendment—with its background of Civil War and Lincolnian dedication to human equality—adds something of import to the general body of regime principles.

Regime principles are also represented in national traditions that reflect our origins and elaborate on them as well. Hence it is often appropriate for the Court to emphasize enduring American standards of value or norms "rooted in the traditions and conscience of our people."[42] But, as the grounds for this emphasis are less clear than they might be, some scrutiny of them is imperative. It is periodically argued that, when the Court focuses on traditional norms (at the expense of efforts to constitutionalize new rights), it is simply following majority opinion. Why should a minority have to give up its claims of right because of a mere opinion that happens to be accepted by greater numbers of people? In response we may argue that this is not, or need not be, an accurate characterization of what is happening. A focus on beliefs that really are "rooted in the traditions of our people" can function as a restraint on judicial aggrandizement. It can do so by ensuring that what the Court does (when lacking precise textual guidance) is in accord with a kind of longstanding or underlying consent of the governed. And, more often than not, customary attitudes with a long history among us can be seen as reflections of regime standards or their moral preconditions. On this view public disapproval of polygamy, pornography, abusive vulgarity in public places, and the like has a status more respectable than that of a mere collection of arbitrary opinions. These are beliefs supportive (however unreflectively) of civilities that republican society needs. Of course, this kind of justification is unavailable for judicial decisions that bow to a currently prevailing opinion simply because it is currently prevailing. If such vulnerable decision making is to be avoided, judges have to be able to distinguish deep-rooted beliefs from ephemeral ones and opinions that are respectable in light of regime considerations from arbitrary or irrational taboos.

I am far from suggesting here that recourse to the ideas of the founding, as amended, and to time-honored public beliefs can conclusively resolve our specific issues concerning the scope and limits of constitutional provisions. No theoretical perspective can substitute for the practical experience and judgment that are always necessary when general principles have to be applied to concrete situations. What we may sensibly seek from such recourse is a basic orientation, a conceptual and moral framework, by which our thinking about those issues may be illuminated. This claim (indeed this whole essay) rests on the presupposition that it makes a difference what orientation to the premises and purposes of liberal democracy is judicially adopted or assumed.[43]

Among the most salutary lessons that jurisprudence can learn from study of our republican regime are lessons about its complexity. As it depends on delicate balances among civic institutions, so too does it depend on delicate balances among principles and purposes. From the *Federalist* we learn that the constitutional design is meant to accommodate diverse elements of the public good—"combining the requisite stability and energy in government with the inviolable attention due to liberty, and to the republican form" and "mingling them together in their due proportions."[44] A sense of proportionality is necessary because the demands of liberty and of stability may be in tension. And the study of our history confirms what Tocqueville so powerfully teaches—that conflicts between claims for equality and claims for liberty are endemic to our kind of society. The same is true of other disparate desiderata of our complex liberal polity—majority rule and property rights, personal liberty and domestic tranquillity, popular government and the rule of law. An approach to adjudication that keeps in mind the pervasive need for accommodation of these diverse regime considerations will be a jurisprudence of moderation. An approach governed by the dignity principle and the new theoretical orientation attending it will not be. The new orientation advances a standard of justice that is at once more egalitarian and more libertarian than our historic one, and it places that standard in a position of ethical sovereignty. Considerations in competition with it are denied moral status. Political concerns and practical judgments about the public good are treated as merely "utilitarian" interests that must give way to the imperatives of justice.[45]

Of course, what is right should normally prevail over what is simply advantageous. But it is an ancient teaching, uncontradicted by modern experience, that political life is largely the sphere of the prudential. Hence the relationship between right and prudence, between the imperatives of principle and the imperatives of social reality, is a problem—it is one of the great problems of moral and political philosophy. In apparent accord with the Rawlsian priority, Aristotle says that "the good in the sphere of politics is justice," but he goes on to say that "justice consists in what tends to promote the common interest."[46] Therefore a conception of justice that disserves the common interest by failing to allow for the preservation of its various components could not be a valid one. The traditional American conception of justice, un-Aristotelian though it is in substance, does allow for the preservation of the various components of our public good.

The Rawlsian theory and the constitutional doctrines generated by it may be viewed as a return to natural right. But this "return" is infused with grand expectations for the reformation of society. It rests on presuppositions about human nature considerably less sober than those on which Lockean natural rights theory rests. The principles of "life, liberty, and property" (or pursuit of happiness) and the institutions that protect them owe less to grand visions of human worth than to realistic assessments of human wants and limitations. Finally our dignity may be best served by a thoughtful realism about our inclinations and possibilities.

Ordered Liberty

We have to acknowledge that, long before the Rawlsians appeared on the scene, classical natural rights philosophy had fallen on hard times in our intellectual circles. Nowadays one scarcely finds any constitutional lawyers or scholars who adhere to it in its entirety. While many of its consequences are still accepted in our law and public opinion, there is much skepticism about its foundations. To deny that this poses a problem of some magnitude would be foolish. But a jurisprudence appropriate for this regime need not depend on entire acceptance of the Lockean foundations. We still have available to us orientations suitable to a jurisprudence of moderation. One of these is the concept of "ordered liberty." That concept made its appearance when Justice Cardozo sought to determine what elements of the Bill of Rights are properly applied to the states through the Fourteenth Amendment. Cardozo maintained that due process incorporates and makes binding on the states only those rights that are "of the very essence of a scheme of ordered liberty."[47]

Of course, "ordered liberty," like "human dignity," is a highly abbreviated connotation of what American constitutional justice is supposed to be about. But it can serve us as a paradigm alternative to the dignity principle. It echoes the founders' aspiration to a system that secures liberty while lawfully restricting abuses of liberty. Insofar as it seeks to accommodate disparate aspects of the public good, ordered liberty reflects the idea of a balanced republic. This paradigm does not confine the judiciary as much as contemporary interpretivists aspire to confine it (the framers had no intention of making *anything* from the Bill of Rights binding on the states). But neither does it encourage the judge to create rights in the process of forging a new moral order. Since it directs the Court to enforce on the states only such norms as are essential imperatives of liberal democracy, it requires judges and citizens alike to reflect on the distinction between rights that are indispensable to our way of life and (putative) rights that are not. While this orientation hardly precludes discretionary judgment, it has little in common with the kind of one-sided moralizing that the dignity principle encourages.

Perhaps there are better ways than the one I have outlined here of conceptualizing an alternative to current interpretivist and noninterpretivist thought about constitutional law and justice. It is to be hoped that the inquiry will be pursued, for neither of these opposing doctrines is able to make satisfactory sense of our constitutional enterprise. And interpretivists are invited to consider, as a practical matter, how unlikely it is that their position will fully prevail; intentions of the framers or not, the Bill of Rights is sure to remain in the Fourteenth Amendment, requiring judicial articulation. And they are invited to consider, as a theoretical matter, that their position is necessarily incomplete. It needs a broadening of horizons.

There is yet another reason to expect that the inquiry will be pursued. The subject of constitutional interpretation, haunted as it is by large questions about law and politics, the lawful and the right, is of inherent philosophic and human interest.

Notes

1. *The Federalist Papers* (New York: New American Library, 1961), p. 471.
2. Ibid., p. 467.
3. Ibid., p. 470.
4. 5 U.S. (1 Cranch.) 137 (1803).
5. 17 U.S. (4 Wheat.) 316 (1819).
6. Id. at 407.
7. Id. at 421.
8. 10 U.S. (6 Cranch.) 87 (1810).
9. Id. at 139.
10. 302 U.S. 319 (1937).
11. 98 U.S. 145 (1879).
12. 268 U.S. 510 (1925).
13. Id. at 535.
14. See Raoul Berger, *Government by Judiciary: The Transformation of the Fourteenth Amendment* (Cambridge, Mass.: Harvard University Press, 1977).
15. Ibid., p. 408.

16. See Alexis de Tocqueville, *Democracy in America* (New York: Vintage, 1945), vol. 1, p. 290.

17. Robert H. Bork, *The Great Debate: Interpreting Our Written Constitution* (Washington, D.C.: Federalist Society, 1986), p. 46.

18. Robert H. Bork, "Foreword" to Gary L. McDowell, *The Constitution and Contemporary Constitutional Theory* (Cumberland, Va.: Center for Judicial Studies, 1985), p. x.

19. Bork, *The Great Debate*, p. 48.

20. *Journals of the Continental Congress*, vol. 1 (1774), p. 108.

21. Robert H. Bork, "Neutral Principles and Some First Amendment Problems," *Indiana Law Journal*, vol. 47 (1971), p. 23. It is noteworthy that the author's commitment to representative democracy is associated with a pronounced moral skepticism that casts doubt on any standards of right except those provided by positive law.

22. *The Federalist Papers*, pp. 314–15.

23. John Locke, *Second Treatise of Government* (Indianapolis: Bobbs-Merrill, 1952), p. 15.

24. Walter Berns, *Taking the Constitution Seriously* (New York: Simon and Schuster, 1987), p. 223.

25. Ibid., pp. 220–25.

26. 98 U.S. 145 (1879).

27. 413 U.S. 49 (1973).

28. It seems to me that Berns's perspective does transcend that mold, critical though he is of "the prevailing view . . . that Supreme Court Justices are not bound by the original understanding of a constitutional provision or by the intent of its framers" (*Taking the Constitution Seriously*, p. 217). He is also critical of the Court for ignoring the lessons of philosophic thinkers, like Tocqueville, on the importance in republics of an ethic of self-restraint and institutions promoting it.

29. Michael Perry, *The Constitution, the Courts, and Human Rights* (New Haven, Conn.: Yale University Press, 1982) p. 111.

30. Ibid., p. 100.

31. Consider Justice William Brennan's widely noted lecture at Georgetown University on October 12, 1985. In a text of thirteen pages the term "dignity" is employed thirty-four times and explicated very little if at all.

32. If the dignity principle (as employed by current advocates) were a genuinely universalizable concept of moral philosophy, it would allow for consideration of the Kantian argument that capital punishment respects the murderer as a rational being by holding him fully responsible for his crime. It would also entertain the idea (held by many citizens) that our common humanity is affirmed by laws that restrict the more degrading forms of obscenity and public vulgarity. Of course, it entertains no such ideas.

33. Ronald Dworkin, *Taking Rights Seriously* (Cambridge, Mass.: Harvard University Press, 1977), p. 269.

34. Ronald Dworkin, "Liberalism," in Stuart Hampshire, ed., *Public and Private Morality* (Cambridge: Cambridge University Press, 1978), p. 137.

35. See John Rawls, *A Theory of Justice* (Cambridge, Mass.: Harvard Univer-

sity Press, 1971), especially, pp. 73–74, 100–104. Rawls evidently believes that all advantages and disadvantages (all inequalities) resulting from differences in human minds and characters are undeserved.

36. *The Federalist Papers*, p. 82.

37. Ibid., p. 387.

38. See Herbert J. Storing, "The Constitution and the Bill of Rights," in Robert A. Goldwin and William A. Schambra, eds., *How Does the Constitution Secure Rights?* (Washington, D.C.: American Enterprise Institute, 1985); and Harry M. Clor, "Reflections on the Bill of Rights," to be published under the auspices of the Center for the Study of the Constitution.

39. Storing, "The Constitution and the Bill of Rights."

40. This point is well argued in Gary J. Jacobsohn, *The Supreme Court and the Decline of Constitutional Aspiration* (Totowa, N.J.: Rowman and Littlefield, 1986).

41. If a specific text is needed in support of this proposition, the best one is *Federalist* No. 51.

42. See Rochin v. California, 342 U.S. 165 (1952); Moore v. East Cleveland, 431 U.S. 494 (1977); Bowers v. Hardwick, 92 L. Ed. 2d 140 (1986).

43. Presumably, this essay will be regarded as a complete failure by anyone who believes not merely that general principles do not decide concrete cases but also that they do not guide judgment. For a forceful argument on the influence of philosophic perspective, see Rogers Smith, *Liberalism and American Constitutional Law* (Cambridge, Mass.: Harvard University Press, 1985).

44. *The Federalist Papers*, pp. 220–27.

45. See Rawls, *A Theory of Justice*, pp. 22–33; and Dworkin, *Taking Rights Seriously*, chaps. 7, 12.

46. Aristotle, *The Politics of Aristotle*, ed. Ernest Barker (New York: Oxford University Press, 1977), p. 129.

47. Palko v. Connecticut, 302 U.S. at 325.

135

A NOTE ON THE BOOK

This book was edited by Trudy Kaplan and Dana Lane
of the publications staff
of the American Enterprise Institute.
The text was set in Palatino, a typeface designed by Hermann Zapf.
Coghill Book Typesetting Company, of Richmond, Virginia,
set the type, and Edwards Brothers Incorporated,
of Ann Arbor, Michigan, printed and bound the book,
using permanent, acid free paper.